IF FOUND:

👤 _____

✉ _____

📱 _____

Greater Than a Tourist Book Series
Reviews from Readers

I think the series is wonderful and beneficial for tourists to get information before visiting the city.

-Seckin Zumbul, Izmir Turkey

I am a world traveler who has read many trip guides but this one really made a difference for me. I would call it a heartfelt creation of a local guide expert instead of just a guide.

-Susy, Isla Holbox, Mexico

New to the area like me, this is a must have!

 -Joe, Bloomington, USA

This is a good series that gets down to it when looking for things to do at your destination without having to read a novel for just a few ideas.

-Rachel, Monterey, USA

Good information to have to plan my trip to this destination.

-Pennie Farrell, Mexico

Great ideas for a port day.

-Mary Martin USA

Aptly titled, you won't just be a tourist after reading this book. You'll be greater than a tourist!

-Alan Warner, Grand Rapids, USA

Even though I only have three days to spend in San Miguel in an upcoming visit, I will use the author's suggestions to guide some of my time there. An easy read - with chapters named to guide me in directions I want to go.

-Robert Catapano, USA

Great insights from a local perspective! Useful information and a very good value!

-Sarah, USA

This series provides an in-depth experience through the eyes of a local. Reading these series will help you to travel the city in with confidence and it'll make your journey a unique one.

-Andrew Teoh, Ipoh, Malaysia

>TOURIST

GREATER THAN A TOURIST- MICHIGAN USA

50 Travel Tips from a Local

L. Smith

Greater Than a Tourist Michigan USA   Copyright © 2018 by CZYK Publishing LLC. All Rights Reserved.

All rights reserved. No part of this book may be reproduced in any form or by any electronic or mechanical means including information storage and retrieval systems, without permission in writing from the author. The only exception is by a reviewer, who may quote short excerpts in a review.

Cover designed by: Ivana Stamenkovic
Cover Image: https://pixabay.com/en/detroit-michigan-detroit-skyline-1919050/

CZYK Publishing Since 2011.

Greater Than a Tourist
Visit our website at www.GreaterThanaTourist.com

Lock Haven, PA
All rights reserved.
ISBN: 9781723981043

>TOURIST

50 TRAVEL TIPS FROM A LOCAL

BOOK DESCRIPTION

Are you excited about planning your next trip?

Do you want to try something new?

Would you like some guidance from a local?

If you answered yes to any of these questions, then this Greater Than a Tourist book is for you.

Greater Than a Tourist- Michigan USA by L. Smith offers the inside scoop on Michigan. I can't even begin to cover within this e-book all that **Michigan, "the Mitten State"**, has to offer and the wonderful places to visit in this beautiful state. Michigan has a heritage of unique culture, a state proud of its maritime history, its railroad, lumber, manufacturing, automobile industry, and tourism history, and so many other things that make it special. This book is but an attempt to convey what a beautiful and historic state that Michigan is and has become for generations of people who call it home. Once you visit Michigan, it stays in your heart. Discover for yourself its beauty and charm.

Most travel books tell you how to travel like a tourist. Although there is nothing wrong with that, as part of the Greater Than a Tourist series, this book will give you travel tips from someone who has lived at your next travel destination.

In these pages, you will discover advice that will help you throughout your stay. This book will not tell you exact addresses or store hours but instead will give you excitement and knowledge from a local that you may not find in other smaller print travel books.

Travel like a local. Slow down, stay in one place, and get to know the people and the culture. By the time you finish this book, you will be eager and prepared to travel to your next destination.

TABLE OF CONTENTS

BOOK DESCRIPTION
TABLE OF CONTENTS
DEDICATION
ABOUT THE AUTHOR
HOW TO USE THIS BOOK
FROM THE PUBLISHER
OUR STORY
WELCOME TO
> TOURIST
INTRODUCTION
1. Michigan, born and raised, proudly my home state
2. Michigan: What a Great Lake State
3. Michigan: Water, Winter, Wonderland
4. Tourist stops, events, festivals, parks, national forests
5. Mackinaw Island
6. Mackinaw City (located at the tip of the LP)
7. Mackinac Bridge - The Labor Day Bridge Walk
8. Saint Ignace (aka St. Ignace) is located in the Eastern UP
9. Sault Ste. Marie, MI, and Sugar Island (Eastern UP)
10. Top of the U.P (tip of the rabbit's ear) Keweenaw Peninsula

11. Eastern UP and Western UP of Michigan
12. TRAVERSE CITY
13. Sleeping Bear Dunes National Lakeshore
14. Tahquamenon Falls - Upper and Lower
15. Indian River Shrine (Cross in the Woods - National Catholic Shrine)
16. Christmas, MI
17. Munising, Munising Falls, Pictured Rocks
18. The Five Great Lakes surrounding Michigan
19. Detroit (Motor City, Motown, and so much more)
20. Dearborn - Home of Greenfield Village and the Henry Ford Museum
21. Flint, MI (Vehicle City)
22. Shiawassee County
23. Holland, MI - Tulip Time is in May each year!
24. Grand Rapids, MI
25. Lansing, MI - The capital of Michigan
26. Hell, MI (Michigan has some unique places)
27. Pellston, MI
28. Frankenmuth, MI - "Oktoberfest and Bronner's"
29. Birch Run, MI, (Saginaw County)
30. Bay City, Midland, and Saginaw, MI - The Tri-Cities
31. Chesaning, MI - Visit the "Chesaning Showboat Park"
32. The Thumb Area

>TOURIST

33. Northern MI Mitten (Lake Huron side)
34. Northern MI Mitten (Lake Michigan side)
35. The Southwest Corner of the state
36. The Middle and South border area
37. The Michigan and Toledo, OH, border area
38. Agriculture
39. Crops
40. Manufacturing, Transportation, Production
41. Mining
42. Fishing
43. Services
44. Industry
45. What famous products came from Michigan?
46. Michigan wine, beer, cider
47. Apples, Blueberries, and Cherries
48. The Top 5 Reasons To Visit Michigan
49. More Michigan-Made Products
50. Michigan Cities with signature food

TOP REASONS TO BOOK THIS TRIP

50 THINGS TO KNOW ABOUT PACKING LIGHT FOR TRAVEL

Packing and Planning Tips

Travel Questions

Travel Bucket List

NOTES

DEDICATION

This book is dedicated to all people who love Michigan. Even if you are not a Michigan native, once you travel or move there, it has a way of becoming home to many people. I am very proud to call myself a Michiganian or a Michigander. I love my birthplace and my home state of Michigan because it is beautiful and unique; there is no other place like it on Earth.

ABOUT THE AUTHOR

L. Smith was born and raised in Michigan and the same for her family. She traversed the state numerous times. As a child, on an extended trip, her family traveled from the bottom of the state all the way to the top of the "rabbit's ear", or better known as the top northern-most point of the UP of Michigan and down again to the lower U.P. hugging the shoreline and visiting family and friends within the interior of the state as well. That year, back in 1967, the trip took most of the summer. They traveled by truck with a camper top and a travel trailer staying in campgrounds caravanning with a group of extended family. It was a once in a lifetime chance and experience that her parents chose to take back then. Her father once mentioned to her that "you have to see your home state first before you see the rest of the country". It was a time when both the LP, aka "the mitten", and UP, aka "the rabbit", were in their "heyday", it was the "golden age" when Michigan had wonderfully popular tourist spots and it was an experience like no other. Growing up in Michigan, she experienced all the state has to offer. As an adult, she continued to travel all over the state spending numerous weekends "Up North" in Michigan.

During her lifetime, she and her family, traveled many times around the Midwest and over to the east coast, and down south. Though on occasion she did travel by airplane for business and pleasure, more than 75 percent of her traveling was by automobile. It is the only way to really see the country. She made more than 40 trips between Michigan, Ohio, and Florida. Always traveling back to Michigan, she and her husband made several return trips, like "Michigan Snowbirds" and down south to Florida. Eventually, in 2013, they permanently relocated to Florida. To this day, when people ask her where she is from, she holds up her hand, "the Michigan mitten", to show them from where she originates in Michigan. As the author has stated about her birthplace, the great State of Michigan has a special place in her heart and will always be home to her family. Nowhere else, will you encounter such a unique state on Earth. There is no other place like Michigan.

L. Smith is a woman who resides in the south but was born and raised in Michigan where she resided all of her life until 2007. After living in Michigan for 50 years, she and her husband moved for a job offer to neighboring Ohio, which was a new adventure where they experienced first-hand the rivalry between

>TOURIST

the two states is historic and very real. For some people, it is a little 'too real". Still, they met many nice people in Ohio. However, they kept returning home to Michigan. She likes to read, write, sew, cook, paint, draw, sketch and on occasion she still enjoys Wilton method cake decorating. For many years of her life she was an avid volunteer and a 4-H Leader who taught sewing, crafts, and Wilton method cake decorating. In recent years, she still enjoys her favorite hobbies. A few years ago, she began relearning Spanish and German. Her heritage is European and her paternal grandparents spoke German which she learned as a child. Originating from the Detroit, Utica, and Shelby Township area of the state her family moved north to the mid-Michigan area, where she spent 43 years of her life splitting time between there and traveling back to the Detroit area.

HOW TO USE THIS BOOK

The Greater Than a Tourist book series was written by someone who has lived in an area for over three months. The goal of this book is to help travelers either dream or experience different locations by providing opinions from a local. The author has made suggestions based on their own experiences. Please do your own research before traveling to the area in case the suggested places are unavailable.

FROM THE PUBLISHER

Traveling can be one of the most important parts of a person's life. The anticipation and memories that you have are some of the best. As a publisher of the Greater Than a Tourist book series, as well as the popular 50 Things to Know book series, we strive to help you learn about new places, spark your imagination, and inspire you. Wherever you are and whatever you do I wish you safe, fun, and inspiring travel.

Lisa Rusczyk Ed. D.
CZYK Publishing

>TOURIST

OUR STORY

Traveling is a passion of the "Greater than a Tourist" series creator. Lisa studied abroad in college, and for their honeymoon Lisa and her husband toured Europe. During her travels to Malta, an older man tried to give her some advice based on his own experience living on the island since he was a young boy. She was not sure if she should talk to the stranger but was interested in his advice. When traveling to some places she was wary to talk to locals because she was afraid that they weren't being genuine. Through her travels, Lisa learned how much locals had to share with tourists. Lisa created the "Greater Than a Tourist" book series to help connect people with locals. A topic that locals are very passionate about sharing.

>TOURIST

WELCOME TO
> TOURIST

INTRODUCTION

The state motto quote shown below may be found on the state flag of Michigan on the seal of the state. On the white ribbon of the seal, is written the quote below.

Seal of Michigan. ... On the white ribbon: Si Quæris Peninsulam Amœnam Circumspice, "If you seek a pleasant peninsula, look about you," which is the official state motto.

Memories of life from childhood to adulthood and seasons spent outdoors in all kinds of weather spring to mind. Summers at night spent chasing fireflies, trips to Bob-Lo Island or "Up North" or family gatherings spent with both friends and family. The fall season brings to mind beautiful falling leaves and jumping in piles of them. My memories include the smell of smoke from a campfire or fireplace on an evening's walk. I still remember a winter's night standing outside at Barbeau, MI, near Sault Ste. Marie, and watching huge white snowflakes fall. It was so quiet and peaceful. During the summer months, I remember riding the waves of the St. Marys River as the freighters went by and waving to the people on deck. Michigan is famous for the song, "The Wreck of the Edmund Fitzgerald" which was sung by Gordon Lightfoot about the sinking of the freighter the SS Edmund Fitzgerald that sank in Lake Superior on November 10, 1975. The entire crew of 29 perished during that fateful storm. I remember visiting Neebish Island, Sugar Island, Ojibwa Island, Sault St. Marie and the Soo Locks, the Au Sable River Cruise, Pictured Rocks, Manistique in Schoolcraft County (Google the Schoolcraft County Historical Society website), and the glass bottom observation raft at Kitchitikipi Springs, Big Spring (Kitch-iti-kipi) in Manistique. Going to Castle Rock and standing next to the big Paul Bunyan and Babe the Blue Ox statues. Visiting the Upper and Lower Tahquamenon falls, aka "Root Beer Falls" near Paradise a stopping at Christmas, MI, and the Mystery Spot near St. Ignace in the UP and numerous places in that area of the state.

>TOURIST

1. MICHIGAN, BORN AND RAISED, PROUDLY MY HOME STATE

My memories are vivid about visiting the Lake of the Clouds and the Porcupine Mountains Wilderness State Park Lookout (observation tower) in the UP and feeling as if I was standing on the top of the world. I loved visiting Mackinaw Island and the Mighty Big Mac, aka the Mackinac Bridge; it is majestic. I remember many hunting and fishing trips, river fishing, smelt dipping, ice fishing, ice-skating, sledding, and tobogganing. What fun we had walking on the Sleeping Bear Dunes, gathering rocks on the shores of Lake Superior, and weekend trips to my parents place at Glennie, MI, or visiting the various state parks and lakes. Good times visiting with family at Utica and Shelby Township. Going to Yates Cider Mill brings back special memories. I remember sledding down the hills, with snow in my face, at Stony Creek State Park near Washington, MI. There were many trips in all seasons all over the state, to name just a few places, such as Traverse City and the Cherry Festival or the Traverse City Zoo. Going to Marquette, Gwynn, Honor, Mio, Rose City, Rifle River Recreation Area, Luzerne, Mack Lake,

McKinley, Glennie, Hale, Oscoda, Ludington, Pentwater, Au Sable, Atlanta, Onaway, Grayling, Gaylord, Pinconning, Frankenmuth, Flint, Lansing, Holland, Stockbridge, Mason, Byron, St. Johns, Birch Run, Clare, Petoskey, Mackinaw City, Saint Ignace. Many trips going "Up North" through Saginaw, Midland, Bay City, Standish, Sterling, Pinconning, Harrisville, Alpena, Long Lake, Au Gres, Aus Sable River, Glennie, Curtisville, Lake City, Cadillac, and Hartwick Pines. Trips all over the state to Goodrich, Almont, Capac, Romeo, Shelby Township, Utica, Port Austin, West Branch, Kalkaska, Waters, Vanderbilt, Port Huron, Detroit, Kalamazoo, Battle Creek, Ann Arbor, Ypsilanti, Grand Rapids, and so many more places. Going swimming in Lake Michigan at night was a special treat after putting up hay all day in the hot summer sun. Canoeing down the Shiawassee River took all day. Going to see a concert at Pine Knob, aka DTE Theater, or visiting Greenfield Village and Huckleberry Railroad or stopping at the Dairy Queen in Rose City on the way to the cabin at Canada Creek Ranch near Atlanta, MI, and going to Hillman and Onaway, on family trips with my husband's family. I have visited all five Great Lakes: Erie, Huron, Michigan, Ontario, and Superior. Michigan has the most shoreline with lighthouses and I have visited many of them. We visited Canada many times via the UP and the LP. Michigan is a beautiful state forever in my heart.

2. MICHIGAN: WHAT A GREAT LAKE STATE

If you live in Michigan, spend some time and visit every Great Lake, Michigan, Huron, Erie, Superior and Ontario. Taste some of the local fish and sample some of the local food dishes. Eat a pasty from the UP, or have a Vernors or an A & W Root Beer float, and eat Mackinaw Island fudge or have a piece of cherry pie from Traverse City. More than 150 movies have been filmed in Michigan, i.e., Gran Torino (Detroit area), An Ordinary Killer is linked to Owosso, and Somewhere In Time (Mackinaw Island), Dream Girls (Detroit), along with many other movies and books. The Bear book and movie is linked to author James Oliver Curwood, Owosso, MI. Another movie linked to Owosso is The Polar Express movie about the Pere Marquette 1225 train along with many more books and movies that originated in Michigan. Do you remember the old Faygo commercials and riding the boat to Bob-Lo Island (Amherstburg, Ontario, Canada)? Well, you can still see the old Bois

Blanc Island (Canada) today (aka Bob-Lo Island). Sorry to say, they lost one of the original boats this year (July 2018), the SS Ste. Claire. The other boat is the SS Columbia. Take the Algoma snow train or take a fall color tour. Go to Frankenmuth during Oktoberfest or visit Mackinaw Island. Visit both the LP and the UP. Are you a Michiganian or a Michigander or a Yooper (above the bridge) or a Troll (under the bridge)? During any season, experience the splendor of this beautiful state exploring the natural beauty and numerous tourist attractions. There is so much beauty, fun, and food to experience there, you will want to stay forever in beautiful "Pure Michigan".

3. MICHIGAN: WATER, WINTER, WONDERLAND

Growing up in Michigan, born there in 1957, I grew up in the 1960's and 1970's, the tourist slogan back then was "Water, Winter, Wonderland". The saying was printed on the license plates, which is why I remember it so well. That and "Smoky the Bear" TV commercials saying, "you too can prevent forest fires". I have always called Michigan, the best all around all-weather and sports state. You can do any sport there from water and snow skiing, to hiking, bike riding, skating, riding motorcycles to playing baseball (a huge Detroit Tigers fan). I support all Michigan teams. Are you a Sparty or a Wolverine (aka the great divide) MSU versus U of M? There are the pro teams of the Detroit Tigers (baseball), the Redwings (ice hockey), the Pistons (basketball), the Detroit Lions (football) and remember the Michigan baseball minor league teams like the Michigan Whitecaps and the Lansing Lugnuts. If hunting and fishing is your sport, Michigan is the best place for it. Do you like camping, hiking, hang gliding, kayaking, canoeing, jogging, walking, biking, (Rails to Trails), swimming, ice skating, rollerblading, skydiving, snowmobiling, fishing (lake, river, stream), ice fishing, swimming, water diving, rope climbing, zip lining, snow skiing or water skiing, wave boarding, surfing, rock climbing, baseball, basketball, hockey, soccer, football or just name your sport and you can do it in Michigan. There is a season for everything sports related in Michigan.

4. TOURIST STOPS, EVENTS, FESTIVALS, PARKS, NATIONAL FORESTS

There are thousands of great tourist stops to visit in Michigan in the UP (Upper Peninsula) and the LP (Lower Peninsula). The whole state is one huge tourist stop. But then, I am biased in that respect. To gain some perspective about the amount of places to visit, Michigan has 101 state parks, 17 state-operated harbors, and 133 state forest campgrounds, and thousands of miles of trails. Some trails can use vehicles and others are just walking or hiking trails. Michigan is part of the Rails to Trails program. I will name a few favorites and popular stops but there are some many great out-of-the-way and uncommon ones to explore as well. Of course the fact that Michigan has the most shoreline with lighthouses is undisputed. So pick a spot and visit a lighthouse. There is the Au Sable and the Ludington lighthouse that are good to visit. Frankenmuth is a must see and of course Mackinaw Island and Fort Mackinaw. But, there is also Fort Wilkins in the UP and how about Whitefish Bay or one of my favorite places is Lake of the Clouds in the Porcupine Mountains in the UP. Do you know that Michigan has five U.S. national forests?

>TOURIST

The Huron National Forest is in the LP, the Hiawatha National Forest (near Manistique in the UP), the Ottawa National Forest is in the UP, and the Manistee National Forest is in the LP along and nearby to the Lake Michigan shore and the Huron-Manistee National Forest in the LP. Holland during the Tulip Festival in May each year is a must do trip. The Kirtland's Warbler (a rare endangered neotropical migrant bird) has made Michigan a nesting ground for many years in several areas of the state. The jack pine nesting areas are near McKinley, Mio, Glennie, Curtisville, and Grayling, MI. The Algoma Snow Train (Agawa Canyon), Algoma, MI, near Sault Saint Marie, MI, has breathtaking views in the winter but also very scenic in any other season. The fall color tours are absolutely beautiful. Just pick a spot during peak viewing times or make a trip from the bottom of the lower LP to the top of the UP during the fall season. You will not be disappointed. During every season, year-round, there are hundreds of festivals, fairs, and events going on. Just search online to find one during any weekend of the year. Some of my favorite festivals are the Traverse City Cherry Festival, the Frankenmuth Oktoberfest, the Holly Michigan Renaissance Festival, the St. John's Mint Festival, the Curwood Festival in Owosso and the

Durand Railroad Days and Corunna Fourth of July Festival and the Shiawassee County 4-H Fair and the Michigan State Fair that used to be held in Detroit is now held in Novi, MI. Also, the Woodward Dream Cruise. I love this unique "gem of a state". There is no other state like it in the USA. No other state has five freshwater lakes and such beautiful landscape. Only in beautiful "Pure Michigan"!

5. MACKINAW ISLAND

Mackinaw Island is a state park and a great place to visit any time of year but most people visit the island in the spring, summer, and fall when the island is open for the tourist season. There are year-round residents who live on the island. Try to go in off-peak times to save a little money on your trip. If you want to stay on the island, reserve a hotel room well in advance of your trip. Riding bikes and carriage rides are fun. Each day of the tourist season, the bikes are quickly reserved so plan ahead to secure a bike to ride for your day trip. Wear a good pair of walking shoes and comfortable clothes because you will be walking a great amount of time on the island. You will ride a ferry to the island. Automobiles for tourists are not allowed on the island. Fort Mackinac is on the island

>TOURIST

and worth visiting. Stop at one of the fudge shops and buy some fudge to take home. There is so much to see and do that it is hard to see it all in just one day. Visit the beautiful Grand Hotel. Unless you are a paying guest, you can only take a picture of it. But, it is worth the view and the visit just to see the Grand Hotel in person. A historic hotel, the movie Somewhere in Time was filmed on Mackinaw Island. It is one of my favorite places to visit in Michigan. Everyone who visits Michigan wants to visit this famous historic island resort which has a Facebook page and video cams to view the island year-round. Once you visit Mackinaw Island, you will want to return every year.

6. MACKINAW CITY (LOCATED AT THE TIP OF THE LP)

Mackinaw City is located on the northern tip of Michigan's Lower Peninsula (LP). This historic city is the site of Fort Michilimackinac, an 18th century fort and fur-trading post, and is also the city where the Mackinac Bridge begins, crosses the Straits of Mackinac, and connects with the Upper Peninsula (UP). Nearby is the Old Mackinac Point Lighthouse, founded in 1889, as well as Wilderness State Park, the Lake Michigan shoreline with plenty of trails and camping sites. Not too far away is Lake Paradise (aka Lake Carp) and French Farm Lake. There are many historic items to view at the fort and lighthouse. When you cross the Mackinac Bridge on the right is Lake Huron and on the left is Lake Michigan. Head southeast of Mackinaw City along the Lake Huron shoreline head south on U.S. 23 to visit Cheboygan, MI, and in between stop at Grand View and Point Nipigon. Or, go west of Mackinac City along the Lake Michigan shoreline and visit the Headlands International Dark Sky Park and farther west is Wilderness State Park. On the Lake Michigan side of the Mighty Big Mac, out in the lake sits Beaver Island. And about one-half hour below the bridge is Indian River and the Indian River Cross in the Woods National Catholic Shrine. Michigan has hundreds of tourist gems such as these places that people miss but those who do stop always want to return again.

>TOURIST

7. MACKINAC BRIDGE – THE LABOR DAY BRIDGE WALK

Visible from the LP and the UP is the Mackinac Bridge lit up at night. A stunning view and special treat that you will want to see and take a few pictures for your album. The bridge construction began in 1954 and it was completed and opened to traffic on November 1, 1957. It measures 26,000 ft. in length and the span is five miles between the LP and the UP. The height is 552 ft. During the Labor Day weekend, the annual bridge walk is a popular historic event with up to 60,000 people from all over the world walking over the Mighty Big Mac's five-mile span between the LP and UP. The annual bridge walk began back in 1958. In 2018, for the 60th year, and for the first time in history, participants will be able to begin their annual trek from Mackinaw City in the LP or from St. Ignace in the UP. Throughout the year, the Mackinac Bridge Authority (MBA) hosts events. Check their website for historic and event information.

8. SAINT IGNACE (AKA ST. IGNACE) IS LOCATED IN THE EASTERN UP

Saint Ignace, MI, is a beautiful city located in the UP at the north end of the Mackinac Bridge. The Straits State Park, is a waterfront beach park with campsites, bridge views, picnic areas, and a playground. Nearby, in St. Ignace is a mix of history and modern convenience with plenty of tourist fun. Each year in July, St. Ignace hosts an annual car show. Thousands of people gather for this annual event. Castle Rock, which rises 195.8 feet (59 m) over the waters of nearby Lake Huron, was created by erosion of surrounding land. After the glacial period, post-glacial Lake Algonquin (now part of Lake Huron) formed. The Ice Age melt-off caused the waters of Lake Algonquin to be higher than what the water level of Lake Huron is today. Over time, the declining water eroded much of the land. Castle Rock, which resisted this erosion, is made of limestone; it is called a sea stack or sea chimney which is similar to several rock formations on nearby Mackinac Island, such as Arch Rock or Sugar Loaf. For generations, local residents have told many stories about Castle Rock and the mythical history of

>TOURIST

it. Of course, there are actual facts about it as well. Historically, it was referred to as "Ojibwa's Lookout", but nearby Rabbit's Back was probably the real lookout point. Rabbit's Back, is a raised peninsula, that extends to Lake Huron and it is located 4 miles (6.5 km) north of St. Ignace in the U.S. state of Michigan. The peninsula separates two bays of the northwestern coast of Lake Huron. Evergreen Shores located to the south and Horseshoe Bay is located to the north. From nearby Mackinac Island the peninsula is said to appear like the back of a crouching rabbit, which is how it garnered the name of Rabbit's Back. The summit of the peninsula is 696 feet (212 meters) above sea level, and 115 feet (35 meters) above the level of nearby Lake Huron. The peninsula is located within Hiawatha National Forest. Statues of Paul Bunyan (lumberjack) and his faithful sidekick, Babe the Blue Ox, greet visitors to Castle Rock, and a nearby gift shop. Back in 1928, C. C. Eby purchased Castle Rock and turned it into a popular public tourist attraction. Generations of tourists visit each year to have their pictures taken standing next to the historic statues. The popular attraction continues to be owned and operated by the Eby family. The attraction open from mid- May through mid-October. An admission fee is charged. Reference of historic facts: Wikipedia

9. SAULT STE. MARIE, MI, AND SUGAR ISLAND (EASTERN UP)

Sault Sainte Marie, MI, located in Chippewa County on northeastern end the UP on the Canadian-USA border. Sault Ste. Marie State Forest Area is approximately 350 miles north of Detroit, MI, and home to the historic Soo Lock system which is part of the St. Lawrence Seaway locks system. Settled long ago by Native Americans, it was a busy trading crossroads for fishing and trading among tribes of the Great Lakes. It became the first European settlement in what later became the Midwest USA. But back in 1668, Father Jacques Marquette, a French Jesuit priest, traveled to the area and founded a Catholic mission. Later French colonists established a fur trading post, which attracted trappers and Native Americans alike. The area prospered and by the late 18th century, it was a well-traveled trading settlement, a 3,000 mile route between Montreal and the land north of Lake Superior. For more than 150 years, the settlement was ruled by the French and later British colonial rule. After the War of 1812, five

>TOURIST

years later, a US–UK Joint Boundary Commission reached a border treaty in 1817 between the Michigan Territory of the USA and the British Province of Upper Canada. After the 1817 treaty, the area was split apart and became twin cities, one half on each side of the U.S. and Canadian border. Sault Ste. Marie, U.S. and Sault Ste. Marie, Canada, were each incorporated as independent municipalities toward the end of the nineteenth century. But, the Saint Lawrence River remained the strong bond between the two countries. While in the area, visit Sugar Island and stay in a quaint cabin along the St. Marys River and also visit the twin city of Sault Ste. Marie, Ontario, Canada, which is another must-see stop on your UP tour. As long as you are already in the UP, visit nearby Canada for a day trip. Before venturing over the border, check ahead for the current U.S. / Canadian border requirements as well as the current rate of exchange. Historical reference facts: Google; Wikipedia

10. TOP OF THE U.P (TIP OF THE RABBIT'S EAR) KEWEENAW PENINSULA

The Keweenaw Peninsula (pronounced KEE-wi-naw), is the northernmost part of Michigan's UP. The land mass juts into Lake Superior and was the site of the first copper (ore) boom in the United States. Rich deposits of copper ore (along with silver deposits) supplied a mining industry during the 19th century and well into the 20th century. Though hard rock mining stopped in 1967, copper sulfide deposits were still found near Ontonagon. The industry was so prevalent that it created a need for mining education which led, in 1885, to the founding of the Michigan Mining School now known as Michigan Technological University (MTU) in Houghton, MI. Along with the copper mining industry, the white pine lumber boom supplied lumber and timbers for mine shafts, as a heating source, and to build homes and buildings. Back then, logging mills operated during the winter months because snow helped to move the logs. Highway US 41 ends in the northern Keweenaw at the Michigan State Park housing Fort Wilkins. Hwy US 41 was locally referred to as the "Military Trail" that started in Chicago in the 1900s

>TOURIST

and ended in the Keweenaw wilderness. The restored fort has numerous historical exhibits. From 1964 to 1971, the University of Michigan cooperated with NASA and the U.S. Navy to run the Keweenaw Rocket launch site. Statistics from the 2000 census, list its population as roughly 43,200. Major industries are logging and tourism, along with jobs related to Michigan Technological University and Finlandia University. Back in history, copper ore mining was an industry in the UP. More than 1 billion years ago, volcanic activity produced lava flows in the Keweenaw Peninsula where lava and native copper can still be found today. The Keweenaw Peninsula and Isle Royale were formed by the Midcontinent Rift System, and are the only sites in the USA with evidence of prehistoric aboriginal mining of copper. Historically recorded are artifacts made from copper by ancient Indians that were traded as far south in the U.S. the state of Alabama. This unique location is where Chlorastrolite (Isle Royale Greenstone), the state gem of Michigan, may be found. The official state stone is the Petoskey Stone (1965).The northern end of the UP is sometimes referred to as Copper Island, or "Kuparisaari", by early Finnish immigrants and it is separated from the rest of the UP by the Keweenaw Waterway which is a natural waterway that was dredged and expanded back in the 1860's between the cities of Houghton (south side – named for Douglas Houghton) and Hancock (on the north side). Tourist stops: Brockway Mountain, Calumet, Copper Harbor, Copper Harbor Lighthouse, Copper Falls, Eagle Harbor and Lighthouse, Bete Grese Preserve, Great Sand Bay, Fort Wilkins Historic State Park and campgrounds, George Hite Dunes and Marsh Preserve, Houghton and Hancock, Keweenaw National Historic Park, Keweenaw Bay, Lake Fanny Hooe, Maclain State Park, Porcupine Mountains Wilderness State Park and Lake of the Clouds Overlook (You will love it.), Ontonagan and numerous other places not listed to be explored. Weather facts: Lake Superior (The Big Lake Gitche Gumee or Big-Sea-Water) significantly affects the climate of the Keweenaw Peninsula. The spring season is cool and short. The summer season has highs near 70 °F (21 °C). Fall starts in September, with the winter season beginning in mid-November. Peak color tours start in late September and run to early October. The Keweenaw Peninsula receives abundant amounts of lake-effect snow from Lake Superior. Annual snowfall reaches 220 inches per winter season in Hancock, MI. Farther north, in Delaware, MI, an unofficial average of about 240

>TOURIST

inches (610 cm) has been recorded. At Delaware, the record snowfall for one season was 390 inches (990 cm) back in 1979. Averages over 250 inches (640 cm) are recorded near the tip of the Keweenaw Peninsula. Popular food items: Pasties, jams, jellies, fish from Lake Superior. Historical facts: Google; Wikipedia

11. EASTERN UP AND WESTERN UP OF MICHIGAN

Some Eastern and Western UP tourist stops have previously been mentioned within other sections of this e-book. However, I will mention a few more below. Eastern UP and nearby regions to visit:

Brimley, Kinross Twp., the former Kincheloe Air Force Base and was built in the UP in 1943 during WWII and it was in service until 1977. It was also known by the former names of Kinross Army Air Field, Kinross Air Field, Kinross Air Force Auxiliary Field, and Kinross Air Force Base. Now in present-day, it is known as Chippewa County International Airport, Kinross Correctional Facility, and the community of Kincheloe located on the site of the former base. Originally, the base was named for Iven Kincheloe (1928 -1958), a test pilot from Michigan.

Other historic sites of interest: Whitefish Bay, Whitefish Point, Bay Mills, Dollar Settlement,Tahquamenon State Park and of course every tourist must see the Upper and Lower Tahquamenon Falls, affectionately dubbed "Root Beer Falls", which are beautiful during any season. But, during the fall season's beautiful autumn leaves and during the winter season snow, they are a sight to

>TOURIST

behold. Visit the historic DeTour, Drummond and Drummond Island, Sault Ste. Marie, the Soo Locks, Soo Junction, Grand Marias, Newberry State Forest Area, Seney, Munising, and Munising Falls. Also visit nearby Hiawatha National Forest, Naubinway, Manistique, Gladstone, Escanaba, Escanaba River State Forest, Marquette, Ishpeming, Gwinn, Gwinn State Forest, KI Sawyer AFB (Built in 1944 and closed in 1995 was repurposed as KI Sawyer International Airport), now visit the KI Sawyer Heritage Air Museum and gift shop.

Western UP: The middle to western UP area covers a large area.

Impossible to list them all, hundreds of interesting tourist spots and towns exist in this part of the UP and the same for the Eastern UP. I cannot list them all but I will mention several of them. Venture up to Isle Royal National Park, which is an island, located northwest of Copper Harbor in Lake Superior. Or visit L'Anse, Barraga State Forest area, Calumet, Ontonagon, Bessemer, Watersmeet, Ironwood, Iron River, Crystal Falls, Iron Mountain, Norway, Marinette, and follow the southern shoreline, along US Highway 2 along Lake Michigan all the way back to the Mighty Big Mac. Back when I was young, my family traveled multiple times all over the UP and LP. When I was older, with my own family, we again traveled all over the UP and on a return trip we followed the Highway 2 route back to the Big Mac. A trip I will always remember.

12. TRAVERSE CITY

Traverse City is located along Grand Traverse Bay which flows into Lake Michigan. Year-round beauty and fun. Popular attractions are the Zoo, the Cherry Festival and the parade (annually held in June), and the beach, too, and make a weekend trip because you will need more than one day to enjoy this city. There are wineries, food dishes infused with cherries, a Victorian-era City Opera House which is the oldest of three remaining in the state. Stay at the Great Wolf Lodge. Take a side trip to the nearby areas of the Platte River, Platte Lake, the Betsie River, Beaulah (Crystal Lake), Arbutus Lake, Interlochen, Leland, Honor, Cadillac, Fife Lake, Torch Lake, Suttons Bay (more wineries), Grand Traverse Bay, and Kalkaska to name just a few of the beautiful spots in that area of the state. My family spent many wonderful vacation days there visiting family and friends during every season of the year.

>TOURIST

13. SLEEPING BEAR DUNES NATIONAL LAKESHORE

Sleeping Bear Dunes National Lakeshore is a Michigan treasure located near Maple City, MI, and part of the U.S. National Park Service with miles of sandy beach and towering bluffs that rise 450 feet above Lake Michigan. Add to that breathtaking scenic views and forests, inland lakes and trails to hike. There is an island lighthouse, small coastal villages, and US Life-Saving Service stations, and tons of maritime, agricultural and recreational history to explore. Of course, there are the dunes to climb. But, did you know that there are new trails to enjoy? Not too far away, out in Lake Michigan are the North and South Manitou Islands. Nearby is Benzonia, Interlochen, Traverse City, Old Mission Point and Old Mission Lighthouse, Lake Leelanau, Empire, Lake Ann, Kewadin, Elk Rapids, Crystal Lake, Frankfort, Elberta, Arcadia, the Arcadia Dunes: The CS Mott Nature Preserve, Bear Lake, Manistee, Scottville, Ludington, Pentwater, Reed City, Muskegon, and Newaygo. Michigan is a treasure that has hundreds of wonderful places to explore and enjoy.

14. TAHQUAMENON FALLS – UPPER AND LOWER

Affectionately dubbed as "Root Beer Falls" by many generations of tourists, (because there are iron and minerals in the water and it resembles flowing root beer), this peaceful place is a popular tourist destination with visitors coming from all over the world. Tahquamenon Falls State Park has waterfalls, hiking trails, scenic views, historic markers with information, gift shops, and it is located near M-123 in Paradise, MI, which is appropriately named, for its stunning beauty and peaceful surroundings. The scenic route is a pleasant drive along M-123 looping from Highway M-28 through Paradise, past the Tahquamenon Falls State Park, going through Newberry, stop by and visit the Crisp Point Lighthouse Historical Society, and back to M-28. Hidden in the forest, the falls and park are along the Tahquamenon River and accessible for all who seek the peace and beauty of the UP. The state park has 52,000 acres stretching over 13 miles of mainly undeveloped state-owned terrain.

Centered in this beautiful state park is the Lower Falls along with the Upper Falls that is known to be one of the largest east of the Mississippi River. The

>TOURIST

Upper Falls span 200 feet wide with a 50 foot drop. More than 50,000 gallons of water per second cascade down the Upper Falls in breathtaking color and glory for all to witness and enjoy. Paved pathways lead from nearby parking lots to the observation platforms nearby to the falls. The viewing platforms are handicap accessible and steps lead to the bottom of the falls where they flow into the Tahquamenon River. There is a 4 mile hiking trail along the river leading to the Lower Falls. For the tourist's convenience there are maps, historic markers with information about the park and falls, a restaurant and a gift shop at the Upper Falls. According to historic facts, originally a logging camp existed in the Upper Falls area and an onsite building is a replica of old logging Camp 33 which has a deck and fireplace with a picnic area to enjoy. There are picnic tables near the trail entrance with handicap accessible restrooms and trails leading to the Upper Falls park area and trails. Reference: Google – Explore the North.com/Tahquamenon

15. INDIAN RIVER SHRINE (CROSS IN THE WOODS – NATIONAL CATHOLIC SHRINE)

Location: 7078 M-68 Indian River, Michigan 49749

Description: Beautiful, peaceful and serene. The site has a beautiful bronze statue and cross. People from all over the world make a special journey to visit the Cross in the Woods Shrine to enjoy the solitude and beauty. Titled as "A Quiet Moment", the shrine is located in the outdoor sanctuary at the National Shrine of the Cross in the Woods which is known to be the world's largest crucifix. Catholics may attend daily and weekend mass onsite. It is open to the public for walks on the church grounds to enjoy the serenity from Dawn to Dusk. On the grounds there is a doll museum, gift shop, and a parish office. There are no fees or admissions but generous donations are always welcomed.

>TOURIST

16. CHRISTMAS, MI

Christmas, MI, est. in 1938 and just 4 ½ miles west of Munising, is located along M-28 on the shores of Lake Superior in the Eastern UP of Michigan between Au Train and close to Munising, MI, and the Pictured Rocks National Lakeshore. Take a cruise to visit them and take some scenic photos. Nearby are the Grand Island Harbor Lighthouse, Furnace Lake, and Bay Furnace Campground. Farther northeast, visit the Grand Marais area. Now, when I was a child, Christmas, MI, was in its popular tourist attraction "heyday" back in the mid 1960s. I remember the town was lit up with Christmas lights in the summer. It was a hub of tourist activity. Today, it is still fun and all about Christmas, interesting, and worth stopping by for a visit. There are still very large Mr. and Mrs. Santa Claus signs and a big Old Lady in the Shoe sign and a big Santa Claus statue for snapping photos. There is a North Pole (a big pole) and examples of street names include: Jingle Bell Lane, Holly Drive, Tinsel Drive, Jingle Bell Way, and Santa Lane. What a fun and beautiful place to visit in any season.

17. MUNISING, MUNISING FALLS, PICTURED ROCKS

National Lakeshore along the shores of Lake Superior are part of the Hiawatha National Forest. Enjoy the Munising Falls visitor center and see the Munising Lighthouse. Here is a wonderful tourist spot to take a cruise, especially during the peak fall color tours to view the falls and the Pictured Rocks. Enjoy the Pictured Rocks cruise for time well spent. Stop by and visit Binsfeld Bayshore Park, Grand Island and visit the Horseshoe Falls and gift shop. There are plenty of restaurants, hotels, camping, hiking, or just enjoy the beauty of Lake Superior.

18. THE FIVE GREAT LAKES SURROUNDING MICHIGAN

These five beautiful freshwater lakes is what gives Michigan part of its unique charm and beauty as well a making it the best state for tourism and any type of outdoor sport that you could possibly imagine. The five freshwater interconnected lakes connect to the Atlantic Ocean via the Saint Lawrence River (Seaway). Though, each lake sits in a separate basin, collectively, they are part of the Great Lakes Basin. The lakes are named: Superior, Michigan, Huron

\>TOURIST

(Michigan-Huron), Erie, and Ontario. They are recorded as the largest group of freshwater lakes on Earth. Lake Superior is the second largest lake in the world. Michigan is the only Great Lake located entirely inside the USA. Lakes Superior, Erie, Huron, and Ontario share water boundaries between the U.S. and Canada. These U.S. states share lake boundaries: Illinois, Indiana, Michigan, Minnesota, New York, Ohio, Pennsylvania, and Wisconsin. Throughout the lakes are 35,000 islands. The largest is Manitoulin Island in Lake Huron also considered as the largest island within an inland body of water in the world. The second largest is Isle Royale in Lake Superior. Both islands contain multiple lakes. The Great Lakes contain several peninsulas including the Door Peninsula, the Peninsulas of Michigan, and the Ontario Peninsula. Smaller peninsulas are the Keweenaw, the Thumb, the Bruce, and the Niagara Peninsula. Large population areas on the peninsulas include Grand Rapids; Detroit; London, Ontario; Hamilton, Ontario; Toronto Ontario. Many canals, rivers, and locks connect the Great Lakes to rest of the world. The Saint Lawrence Seaway connects with the Great Lakes Waterway which makes the Great Lakes accessible to ocean vessels. The Chicago River and the Calumet River connects the Great Lakes

Basin to the Mississippi River through a system of man-made canals. The Saint Marys River and the Soo Locks connect Lake Superior to Lake Huron. The Straits of Mackinaw connect Lakes Michigan and Huron. The St. Clair River connects Lake Huron to Lake St. Clair. The Detroit River connects Lake St. Clair to Lake Erie. The Niagara River, including Niagara Falls, connects Lake Erie to Lake Ontario. The Saint Lawrence River and the Saint Lawrence Seaway connect Lake Ontario to the Gulf of St. Lawrence, which connects to the Atlantic Ocean. Historical Reference: Google and Wikipedia

19. DETROIT (MOTOR CITY, MOTOWN, AND SO MUCH MORE)

Detroit is the home of the Detroit Tigers, Lions, Pistons, and the Redwings which are my favorite pro sport teams. Remember too that Michigan has many college teams. In Michigan, the two college rivals, aka the great divide, are U of M and Michigan State. The other well known college rival is Ohio State (OSU). Everyone knows that both MSU and U of M like to beat OSU. Just a bit of friendly rivalry between MI and OH which is a rivalry that dates back more than 150 years. Detroit has culture, food, music,

>TOURIST

art, cars, great sports teams, and much more. My family originates from Detroit (Utica / Shelby Township) and the surrounding suburbs. I love and miss Detroit and all it has to offer. You must visit there to see some unique things not found elsewhere. Like the huge Detroit Pistons basketball in the River Rouge area just off of I-75 or go to a Detroit Tigers game at Comerica Park or visit the Central Market or the State Fairgrounds. Go to the Woodward Dream Cruise. Visit the Fox Theatre and see the Giant Uniroyal tire that sits off of Interstate 94 (Allen Park) between the Southfield Freeway and the Outer Drive. Originally, the giant tire was created by the Uniroyal Tire Company for the 1964 New York Worlds Fair as a functioning Ferris wheel standing approximately 86 ft. tall. Since 1966, it has been a permanent display in Allen Park, MI. From 1964 to 1990 it was owned by Uniroyal. Since 1990, to current, it has been owned by Michelin. Over the years, it has been refurbished. May 2015, marked the 50th anniversary.

20. DEARBORN – HOME OF GREENFIELD VILLAGE AND THE HENRY FORD MUSEUM

Dearborn is a diverse cultural city with many interesting places to visit. Highlight tourist spots: The Henry Ford Museum; Automotive Hall of Fame; Detroit Institute of the Arts; Detroit Zoo; Ford Field; Comerica Park; Detroit Casinos; University of Michigan, Dearborn. Nearby are Rouge Park, Dearborn Heights, Livonia, Westland, Wayne, Allen Park, Lincoln Park, Taylor, Ecorse, Garden City, Inkster, and Melvindale with lots of shopping, food, airports, and much more. Food: Arabic, Middle Eastern, Lebanese, Cuban, Italian, Czech, Slovak, and American, along with many other types of ethnic foods, even BBQ.

Trivia: Greenfield Village has 240 acres of land with 90 acres used for the village attraction and the rest is comprised of forest, river and pasture for the sheep and horses. Side trip tour: Ford Rouge Factory Tour

>TOURIST
21. FLINT, MI (VEHICLE CITY)

Flint, MI, is the largest city and the county seat of Genesee County, MI.

The city is located 66 miles northwest of Detroit, MI, and sits along the Flint River within the Mid-Michigan region of the state. The city was settled in 1819 and incorporated in 1855. During the 19th and 20th centuries, Flint was a leading manufacturing center for carriages and later automobiles where it earned the name of "Vehicle City". General Motors (GM) was founded in Flint in 1908 where it grew into a vital auto industry leader. Throughout the years, with several economic ups and downs, Flint has remained strong within the Mid-Michigan area. The Saginaw Valley area, including Flint, is considered to be one of the oldest continually inhabited areas of Michigan. Flint has a cultural and industrial history with a diverse ethnic culture gathering people from all over the country and the world to this city. Several colleges and universities have campuses within the city and surrounding region. It has municipal services typically offered by large cities, i.e., police, fire, emergency personnel, newspapers and magazine publications, radio and TV stations, hospitals and medical facilities, public transportation, bus stations, railroad, major highways, an airport, shopping, restaurants, museums, a planetarium, orchestras, libraries, sports events, music, arts, movie theatres, golf courses, shopping centers, restaurants, nature areas, hiking, all types of sports, and it hosts several annual events. Several films and movies have been filmed in Flint, MI. Nearby are the communities of Swartz Creek, Fenton, Argentine, Flushing, Linden, Clio, Davison, Montrose, Goodrich, Grand Blanc, Beecher, Burton, Holly, Rankin, Mt. Morris, Otisville, Lennon, Gaines, Owosso, Corunna, Durand, Vernon, Byron, Bancroft, Gaines, Ortonville, Metamora-Hadley, New Lothrop, Columbiaville, Otisville, Birch Run, Frankenmuth, Saginaw, Midland, and many more cities and small towns nearby. Tourist spots: Huckleberry Railroad and Crossroads Village, Flint Institute of Arts, Longway Planetarium, Sloan Museum, Flint Children's Museum, For-Mar Nature (hiking trails), Flint Cultural Center, U.S. 23 Drive-In Theater, Flint Farmer's Market, Whaley Historic House and Museum, and Whiting Auditorium. Food: Italian, Chinese, Mexican, Seafood, Pizza, Barbecue, Middle Eastern, and more. Events: "Back to the Bricks"(car show and cruise), Michigan Renaissance Festival, car

>TOURIST

shows, music, art, food, run / walk events, concerts, ballet, festivals, craft shows, and many more events.

22. SHIAWASSEE COUNTY

Visit the many beautiful cities and towns located in this county, i.e., Owosso (largest city), Corunna, Durand, Vernon, Byron, New Lothrop, Perry, Morrice, Laingsburg, Bancroft, Lennon, and many more small towns located in this county. It is a beautiful county where the Shiawassee River flows. Visit the Durand Union Station, a historic train station, or visit the Steam Railroading Institute in Owosso, home of the Pere Marquette 1225 train, aka "The Christmas Train", that was a part of "The Polar Express" movie and book. Ride the Christmas Train, the 1225, from Owosso to Chesaning to Santa's Village and workshop at the Saginaw County Fairgrounds. Visit the Curwood Castle in Owosso on the banks of the Shiawassee River and go to the Curwood Festival and parade held annually in June. Visit the Shiawassee County 4-H Fair usually held during early August each year. Go to Railroad Days in Durand in May or visit the big Labor Day car show in early September in Durand. Visit the big July 4th Festival, car show, and fireworks in Corunna. This county has good people, good food, and fun festivals year-round. There many interesting historic sites, art festivals, antiques, good restaurants, and much more to see and do all year and in any season of the year. A favorite place to eat in Owosso is Greg & Lou's, O Town Café, Val's Pizza, BJ's Fine Foods, Lula's Louisiana Cookhouse, Johnny V's Smokehouse, El Potrero Mexican Restaurant, Mancino's, Big John Steak & Onion, Itsa Deli Thing, Bentley Grill, Fortune House, Jumbo's Bar & Grill, South 401, and Wrought Iron Grill. There are many more good places to eat in Owosso and the surrounding communities. Try Nick's Hometown Grill in Durand, MI. Visit neighboring Genesee County (Flint and Swartz Creek), Clinton County (Ovid, Elsie, and St. Johns) and Saginaw County (visit the Chesaning Showboat) for food, festivals, and interesting places to visit.

>TOURIST

23. HOLLAND, MI – TULIP TIME IS IN MAY EACH YEAR!

Holland is so beautiful when the tulips bloom in May. You will love the thousands of colorful tulips growing all over the city. Holland is a unique city located on the shore of Lake Macatawa, in Michigan. The Big Red Lighthouse stands by the channel that connects this Lake Macatawa to Lake Michigan. The Holland State Park shelters deer and migratory birds. Ride their cycling trails and watch beautiful sunsets along Lake Michigan. Windmill Island Gardens is where De Zwaan, a centuries-old windmill, is located. The Tulip Time Festival annually held in May, recalls Holland's Dutch roots. Visit Windmill Island Gardens and nearby Ottawa Beach, Holland State Park, Macatawa Yacht Club, Historic Van Raalte Farm Park, and Nelis' Dutch Village theme park celebrating the Netherlands with a wooden shoe factory, cheese-making and a petting zoo. Visit De Klomp Wooden Shoe and Delftware Factory and watch them make wooden shoes and purchase a pair of wooden shoes as a souvenir of your visit. The Holland Bowl Mill is an interesting stop for your itinerary. Eat at the Wooden Shoe Restaurant. There is camping (Oak Grove Resort Campground) and plenty of hotels and restaurants, parks, and tourist shops with souvenirs and the West Michigan Regional Airport is nearby. Stop by Tunnel Park to see the unique beach tunnel. Farther south is Saugatuck Dunes State Park. Hop on I-196 (Gerald R. Ford Freeway) for a quick ride to nearby shops and restaurants or take a side trip to Zeeland or Grand Rapids, MI, home of former U.S. President Gerald R. Ford. There is so much more to see and do in Holland that is not listed here. Explore Holland and enjoy!

Historical Reference: Wikipedia

24. GRAND RAPIDS, MI

Resting place and childhood home of U.S. 38th President Gerald R. Ford (deceased: 2006). Grand Rapids located on the Grand River, just east of Lake Michigan. The Frederik Meijer Gardens & Sculpture Park has a tropical conservatory and multiple gardens. Its art collection includes works by Auguste Rodin, Henry Moore and Ai Weiwei. Downtown, the Grand Rapids Art Museum spotlights Michigan artists in its rotating shows. Grand Rapids has many breweries. Visit the John Ball Zoological Garden and Zoo, the Grand Rapids Public Museum and Planetarium, the Millennium Park, the Gerald R. Ford Library and

>TOURIST

Museum is located in Grand Rapids and in Ann Arbor, MI. Visit the Grand Rapids Children's Museum, Urban Institute for Contemporary Arts, Heritage Hill Historic District, TreeRunner Grand Rapids Adventure Park, Rosa Parks Circle, Grand Rapids African American Museum and Archives, Nishnabe Gemaw Statue, Reeds Lake, Fifth Third Ball Park, catch a Michigan Whitecaps baseball game, or go to a festival or concert. Visit the Meyer May House designed by Frank Lloyd Wright or view La Grande Vitesse which is an abstract red sculpture created by Alexander Caulder in 1969. Spend the day with family enjoying the great park system in Grand Rapids. Catch your flight from the Gerald R. Ford International Airport. Or, if you are driving, head west on I-96 to the state capital of Lansing, MI, and along the way discover many small charming towns to visit and stop for a bite to eat. There are many more interesting places to visit in Grand Rapids, spend a weekend and explore all this unique city has to offer.

25. LANSING, MI – THE CAPITAL OF MICHIGAN

Dating to the 1870s, the Michigan State Capitol building features a cast-iron dome. Tour the Michigan capitol building located on Capitol Avenue. Lansing has many great places to visit, eat and shop. There is a wonderful parks system with nice libraries, public transportation, golf courses, fine dining, fast food, unique cultural food. There are tons of things to see and do there. Lansing is situated along two intersecting rivers, the Grand River and the Red Cedar River. Take a cruise on the Grand River aboard the Michigan Princess Riverboat which is a large double-deck paddlewheel boat. You will love cruising, day or night, the Grand River while you enjoy food and music. Go to a Lansing Lugnuts baseball game or visit the museum, planetarium, the Michigan Historical Museum, Sleepy Hollow State Park (near Ovid, MI). Or, visit the Kresge Museum or the MSU campus dairy store. There is also an MSU Dairy Farm and a processing plant. Spend a day at the Michigan History Center. Take a side trip to Anderson Nature Farm in Delta Township. Lansing is home to the Spartans of Michigan State University. Visit the Turner-Dodge House & Heritage Center,

>TOURIST

Durant Park, Rotary Steam Clock, Cooley Law School Stadium, the MSU Spartan Stadium, Grand Woods Park, Old Town Lansing, River Trail (hiking), Woldumar Nature Center, The Creole Gallery, Carl G. Fenner Nature Center, Brenke Fish Ladder, Jack Breslin Student Events Center, and the Greater Lansing Visitors Center. The Impression 5 Science Center has interactive displays. The collection at the R.E. Olds Transportation Museum includes classic and contemporary Oldsmobile cars. The Potter Park Zoo houses endangered and threatened species such as Magellanic penguins, black rhinos and golden lion tamarins. Throughout the year, Lansing is host to numerous concerts, i.e., Common Ground Music Festival, and numerous events. A favorite event is the East Lansing Arts Festival. If you like antiques, Lansing is the place to go for finding unique artifacts. Michigan has hundreds of places to find antique treasures and craft festivals. There is so much to see and do in Lansing that you will need to spend a few days to enjoy the state capital of Michigan. Explore the outlying areas like East Lansing, Dewitt, Mason, Holt, Delhi Charter Township, Meridian Charter Township, Oneida Charter Township, Onondaga, Bath Township, Shaftsburg, Windsor Charter Township, Eaton Rapids, Eagle, Portland, Watertown

Charter Township, Haslett, Potterville, Grand Ledge, Charlotte, Olivet, Mulliken, Sunfield, Williamston, Dansville, Leslie, Webberville, Fowlerville, Howell, Chelsea / The Purple Rose Theatre, Stockbridge, or go to Uncle John's Cider Mill near St. Johns, MI. There are hundreds of wonderful places to visit within the surrounding region. Explore, discover, and enjoy!

26. HELL, MI (MICHIGAN HAS SOME UNIQUE PLACES)

"Hell, MI, is an unincorporated community, est. 1830s, in Putnam Township, Livingston County, MI. There are two local theories for the origin of Hell's name (aka Hiland Lake, MI)." "The first is that a pair of German travelers stepped out of a stagecoach one sunny afternoon in the 1830s, and one said to the other, "So schön hell!" (translated as, "So beautifully bright!") Their comments were overheard by some locals and the name stuck." "Soon after Michigan gained statehood, George Reeves was asked what he thought the town he helped settle should be called and replied "I don't care. You can name it Hell for all I care." The name became official on October 13, 1841. The second theory is tied to the "hell-like" conditions encountered by early explorers including mosquitoes,

>TOURIST

thick forest cover, and extensive wetlands. It has frequently been noted on lists of unusual place names." "In the early 1930s, the Pinckney, Michigan postmaster W. C. Miller began to receive requests from stamp and postmark collectors for cancellations: Hell had no post office, instead being served by the one for Pinckney, three miles away. On July 15, 1961, a postal substation was established at Hell, operating from May 1 through September 30." "It remains at the back of the general store, although the United States Postal Service does not recognize Hell as a town; it instead uses the name of nearby Pinckney as the mailing address. The community is near the border with Washtenaw County approximately 15 miles northwest of Ann Arbor." What draws people to Hell, MI? Well…of course, it's the unusual name. People love to go there just to say they "went to Hell and back", funny but it's true. They buy unique souvenir items, i.e., T-shirts, etc. It's just a fun tongue-in-cheek tourist thing to go there. While there, visit the surrounding region and go to Pinckney, Halfmoon Hills, Halfmoon Lake, and visit the Pinckney Recreation Area. Go to nearby Kaiserville, Unadilla, and Williamsville. There are many lakes in the region, i.e., Joslin Lake, North Lake, South Lake, Blind Lake, Bruin Lake, Sullivan

Lake, Portage Lake, Silver Lake, and many more lakes. Visit the Unadilla State Wildlife Area. For hiking, try the Waterloo-Pinckney Trail. There are plenty of places to eat and stay overnight and just enjoy the area. Remember to stop and purchase your unique Hell, MI, souvenir. Reference: Google; Wikipedia

27. PELLSTON, MI

Pellston is known as the coldest spot in the state. Brrr! It's motto is "The Icebox of the Nation" shown on the village's welcome sign. In 1933, Pellston recorded the states record low temperature of -53 °F (−47 °C). That's mighty cold! Every year Pellston is regularly spotlighted in national weather reports along with towns like Big Piney, WY and Fraser, CO, and International Falls, MN, as the coldest places in the nation. Pellston is a pleasant, but "cool", village in Emmet County, with 1.91 sq. miles of land, located 18 miles south of Mackinaw City and the Big Mac Bridge. The 2010 census recorded the population as 822. The village lies on the boundary between the Maple River and McKinley Townships on US Hwy 31 and about 10 miles from I-75 and is home to the Pellston Regional Airport. Petoskey is about 20 miles

>TOURIST

to the southwest. The University of Michigan Biological Station is on nearby Douglas Lake. When you visit, stop by the Pellston Historical Society and Museum. This small village, and the surrounding area, has much to offer. There are hotels, gas stations, the Pellston General Store (for bus (Greyhound) and Amtrak train tickets) at the BP Gas Station 45 South US Hwy 31. There are several restaurants, retail stores, churches, antiques, medical and dental offices, animal care, childcare, schools, and collectibles, a converted historic railroad station (antiques shop). Nearby is Lake Kathleen, Burt Lake, Douglas Lake, Munro Lake, Mullett Lake, and the Phillip J. Braun Nature Preserve, Veterans Memorial Park, and the Bryan Wildlife Nature Preserve. Pellston has a diverse culture with good food and interesting places to visit like the Pellston Pioneer Park. Attend the Pellston Village Memorial Festival (summer). Take a side trip and visit the Maple Bay State Forest near Brutus, MI. If you haven't visited Pellston, MI, this "cool village", it is a must-see tourist stop.

Online at: http://www.pellstonmi.com/events.html
Reference: Wikipedia

28. FRANKENMUTH, MI – "OKTOBERFEST AND BRONNER'S"

I love this place, but then, who doesn't? Frankenmuth is fun, beautiful, quaint, historic, and famous for its chicken and Bavarian-style architecture. Visit the Frankenmuth Historical Museum and learn about the area's German roots. Stop by the Michigan's Military & Space Heroes Museum which displays flight gear, Medals of Honor and military equipment. Frankenmuth is bordered by the Cass River and Heritage Park that has an event pavilion and a riverside pathway. There is a covered bridge which is great for family photo ops. The Lager Mill has a museum tracing the city's brewing history. With so many tourist activities and events year-round in this city, too many to list, here are a few places and events to visit. You must go to Frankenmuth's annual "Oktoberfest", a Bavarian Festival event, or take a carriage ride or take a cruise on the Bavarian Belle which is a large paddlewheel river boat. Everyone likes to eat at Zehnder's and the Bavarian Inn restaurants.

Year-round Frankenmuth hosts festivals and events which bring people from all over the world to

>TOURIST

this quaint riverfront community. There are events for the health and fitness buffs like running events, bike races and a triathlon and many events like Summer Music Fest that combine two of Frankenmuth's favorites; music and beer!" All year, there are festivals, classic car shows, i.e., an 80's festival, events for dogs, hot air balloon rides, a huge Snow Festival, Auto Fest, Country Music event, Big Block Party on Main Street, add many wonderful events like colonial encampments, dinner shows and shopping events. From September to mid-October there is a weekly Farmer's Market, and take the Haunted Frankenmuth Walking Tour. Every Friday, from Memorial Day to Labor Day (May 25 – August 31), Main Street comes alive from 6pm – 9pm with live music and street performers. If you love shopping, remember to visit Bronner's Christmas Wonderland located on Christmas Lane in Frankenmuth, MI. Founded in 1945 by Wally Bronner, sadly he passed away in 2008, but he is remembered as building the world's largest Christmas store that greets millions of visitors per year from all over the world. Thanksgiving weekend is the busiest time with well over 50,000 visitors each year for just that weekend. Spend hours roaming through the Christmas trees, collectibles, and gift shops. Bronner's has more than

50,000 decorations, ornaments, trees, hundreds of miles of Christmas lights, and anything Christmas related that you can imagine. Buy a personalized ornament for your Christmas tree. "Bronner's holds exclusive rights to sell Precious Moments Christmas-themed figurines." "Each year, approximately 600,000 glass ornaments, 530,000 feet (161,000 m) of garland, 150,000 postcards and 86,000 light sets (nearly 530 miles (850 km) of light cords) are sold." "With the government of Austria's permission and in keeping with the German theme of Frankenmuth itself, Bronner's built a replica of the Oberndorf, Austria, Silent Night Memorial Chapel in 1992 as a tribute to the Christmas hymn "Silent Night". Year-round, it is a wonderful place to visit. Frankenmuth has it all, shopping, stores, food, hotels, and every convenience nearby that you could ever want. Michigan has hundreds of "gems" to explore and Frankenmuth is definitely one of the best! Reference: Wikipedia

>TOURIST

29. BIRCH RUN, MI, (SAGINAW COUNTY)

Birch Run, MI, (Saginaw County) is a pleasant looking community, where Silver Creek meanders through the community. It is located 15 minutes southeast of Frankenmuth, MI, along I-75 / US 23 and just 22 miles north of Flint, MI. "Birch Run was established in 1852 as a station on the Pere Marquette Railroad. This community has the Birch Run Premium Outlets which opened in 1986 and has grown to beyond mega-shopping and it is the largest outlet mall in the Midwest! The outlet mall has 108 stores and 3 restaurants on the property. It is a great place to spend time for fun and shopping. Convenience galore best describes the plethora of hotels, restaurants, retail stores, plus an entire thriving community. The village is located within Birch Run Township." Along the Dixie Highway is the Birch Run Speedway and Event Center. The Birch Run community host events, festivals, and it has good restaurants and interesting places to visit. Stop by Wilderness Trails Zoo (open from May to October). In 2018, the 1st Annual Dixie Summer Fest (June) was hosted by the Birch Run Bridgeport Chamber of Commerce. Nearby communities: Saginaw, Clio,

Chesaning, Flint, St. Charles, North Branch, Vassar, and farther north are Midland and Bay City.

30. BAY CITY, MIDLAND, AND SAGINAW, MI – THE TRI-CITIES

The Saginaw-Midland-Bay City combined area is a United States metropolitan area defined by the federal Office of Management and Budget (OMB) surrounding the Saginaw Bay and Saginaw River. The region is a part of the larger area known as Mid-Central Michigan which includes the smaller areas of Saginaw, Midland, and Bay City. What makes this area unique? The Saginaw Bay and the Saginaw River anchor these communities. The Saginaw, Tittabawassee, and the Shiawassee Rivers meet, along with the nearby Cass River, near the Shiawassee National Wildlife Refuge. This area is unique because of these river and bay communities. Also, the interesting attractions and events along with great ethnic food (Chinese, Italian, Irish, Polish, German, Indian, Mexican) along with great local seafood make it a great area to visit. There are concerts, healthy outdoor events, museums, all types of sports, fishing, hiking and nature trails, movie theatres, and hundreds

>TOURIST

of activities. Collectively and separately, the Tri-Cities area is a great place to visit. Several large corporations are located in the Tri Cities Region. For example, the Michigan Sugar Company cooperative is owned by 1,250 farmers. It operates a factory and has its headquarters in Bay City. General Motors Corporation operates Powertrain facilities in Flint, Bay City, and Saginaw. The Dow Chemical Corporation's world headquarters is located in Midland. Nexteer Corporation operates Saginaw Steering Systems in Saginaw. The S.C. Johnson and Son Company's manufacturing facility is located in Bay City making Ziploc products. There are several local TV and radio stations. Several newspapers and lifestyle magazine are based in the area, i.e., The Saginaw News, the Bay City Times and the Midland Daily News are available as well as the Great Lakes Bay (a Regional Lifestyle Magazine). Tourism embodies a large part of the local economy. A popular spot along I-75 for "Up North" bound visitors is the outlets at Birch Run. Also, nearby Frankenmuth attracts year round visitors. In between Saginaw and Bay City is the city of Zilwaukee is located nearby to Zilwaukee Township in Saginaw County. Other nearby communities include Freeland, Kochville, Bridgeport, Carrollton, Buena Vista, Hemlock, St.

Charles, Thomas Township, Sanford, Porter, Ryan, Larkin, Willard, Williams Charter Twp., Auburn, Vassar, Millington, Brant, Merrill, Hemlock, Chesaning, Portsmouth, University Center, Richville, Reese, Monitor Twp., Hampton Twp., Tittabawassee Twp., to name a few. Farther north, stop by and visit the communities of Linwood, Kawkawlin, Essexville, Bangor Charter Township, Tobico Marsh Nature Area, Beaver, Almeda Beach, and Pinconning (buy some Pinconning Cheese) on your way "Up North". When you travel farther north, follow the coastline of Lake Huron and visit, Standish, Sterling, Au Gres, Tawas, Oscoda, Harrisville, Hubbard Lake, Barton City, Alpena, Rogers City, Harbor View, Lachine, Posen, Huron Beach, High Banks, Cheboygan, Onaway, Atlanta, Canada Creek Ranch, Hillman, Mio, Luzerne, Grayling, Gaylord, Waters, Vanderbilt, Arbutus Beach, Hartwick Pines State Park, Higgins and Houghton Lake. There is an endless list of great places to visit in Michigan. I wish I could list each and every one of them.

>TOURIST

31. CHESANING, MI – VISIT THE "CHESANING SHOWBOAT PARK"

Chesaning is a village in Chesaning Twp, Saginaw County, Michigan. What is there to see in Chesaning? Spend the day at Chesaning Showboat Park and take a cruise on the Chesaning Showboat called "The Shiawassee Queen". During the summer, thousands of people attend from all over the to watch top-notch entertainers perform at nightly concerts during Showboat Festival Week. There are lots of fun things to see and do, like the 5K run and the 5K Walk. Year-round events and festivals are held in Chesaning. At Christmas, it is all "decked out" in holiday splendor. Take a carriage ride or attend the Candlelight Walk or the Festival of Trees. There is a campground nearby. Eat at the Showboat Restaurant. For many years, Chesaning has hosted an annual (July) car show that draws people from all over the state. Chesaning has a diverse ethnic population and like most areas there is tasty ethnic food available to eat at local popular restaurants. Nearby are many great communities, like Birch Run, Clio, Flint, Frankenmuth, Owosso, Corunna, Montrose, New Lothrop, Flushing, Brant, Ashley, St. Charles, Chapin, Oakley, Henderson, New

Haven, and Juddville. Enjoy live music, great food and atmosphere, and fun in Chesaning, MI.

32. THE THUMB AREA

Port Austin and Grind Stone City sit at the tip of the thumb of Michigan. Nearby are Caseville, Kinde, and Port Hope. Farther south are Filion, Rapson, Harbor Beach, Bay Port, Pigeon, Elkton, Bad Axe, Helena, Sebewaing, Kilmanagh, Owendale, Ubly, Ruth, White Rock, Unionville, Gagetown, Cass City, Austin Center, Minden City, Palms, Forestville, Forester, and Deckerville. Farther south is Port Sanilac, Sandusky, Carsonville, Kingston, Caro, and Marlette. There are many more wonderful communities that make up this area of the state. The Thumb is a region and a peninsula historically named because the Lower Peninsula is shaped like a mitten. The Thumb area is considered to be in the Central Michigan region, located east of the Tri-Cities, and north of Port Huron, Marysville, St. Clair, Marine City, Algonac, Mt. Clemens, St. Clair Shores, Hamtramck, and Metro Detroit. Travel farther inland to visit Utica, Shelby Twp., Sterling Heights, Harrison Charter Twp., Clinton Twp., Fraser, Macomb, Washington Twp., Waldenburg, Fraser,

>TOURIST

Ferndale, Warren, Stoney Creek Metropark, Rochester, Rochester Hills, Troy, Southfield, Livonia, Auburn Hills, Pontiac, Highland Park, Gross Pointe, Gross Pointe Farms, Harper Woods, Eastpointe, Berkley, Birmingham, Farmington Hills, Franklin, Dearborn Heights, River Rouge, Taylor, Westland, and many more great communities that comprise this area of the state. Tourist spots: There are thousands of them in the Thumb region and within the inland communities and greater Detroit area. If you have time, visit Port Austin and Grind Stone City, The Blue Water Bridge area, the Fort Gratiot Lighthouse, and the Thomas Edison Depot Museum. Food: Of course, there's seafood all along the coast line, and wonderful ethnic foods and great restaurants, shopping, year-round events in all four seasons to enjoy in The Thumb Area of Michigan!

33. NORTHERN MI MITTEN (LAKE HURON SIDE)

Interesting historic trivia: Because of its recognizable shape, the Lower Peninsula (LP) is nicknamed "the mitten", with the eastern region identified as "The Thumb". This has led to several folklore myths for the area, one being that it is a hand print of Paul Bunyan (and Babe the Blue Ox), a giant lumberjack and popular European-American folk character in Michigan. Dating as far back as the late 1800s, when asked where they live, LP residents may hold up their right palm and point to a spot on it to indicate the location. The Northern LP is sparsely populated and largely forested and the Southern LP is largely urban or farmland. Yoopers (UP residents) jokingly refer to LP residents as "flat-landers" or "trolls" because they reside south, or under, the Mackinac Bridge.

So what interesting tourist spots are there to see on the Lake Huron side? From Atlanta, Hillman, Clear Lake State Park, Canada Creek Ranch, to Posen, Rogers City (world's largest limestone quarry), Indian River (National Catholic Shrine), Cheboygan, and Mackinaw City. The Lake Huron side has many beautiful vistas and interesting tourist spots, i.e., numerous lighthouses to visit, wonderful nature trails, the Indian River National Catholic Shrine (Cross in the Woods), the Atlanta State Forest Area and the Gaylord and Grayling State Forest Areas. Near Atlanta, MI, the Montmorency County seat, there is a large Elk population. Also, near Gaylord in the Pigeon River State Forest region. There are Whitetail

>TOURIST

deer, bear, and abundant wildlife to see. In fact in parts of the Northern LP "mitten" and the UP there are Elk and Moose in the UP. If you seek peace and absolutely beautiful views of nature, this is the place to go, especially, during the fall months of the color tour. It is so pretty when it snows in the winter. Along with beautiful terrain, there is plenty of outdoor sports, like downhill skiing, cross country skiing, kayaking, hiking, canoeing, fishing, hunting, boating, swimming, camping at numerous state parks, golf, as well as indoor entertainment with great restaurants, festivals, music, and activities for any season of the year.

34. NORTHERN MI MITTEN (LAKE MICHIGAN SIDE)

From Mackinaw City over to Beaver Island, Hog Island, High Island, Garden Island, North Fox Island, South Fox Island, North Manitou Island, South Manitou Island, and Petoskey, Lake Charlevoix, Walloon Lake, Little Traverse Bay, Bellaire, Boyne City, Boyne Falls, Traverse City, Leland, Lake Leelanau, Grand Traverse Bay, Sutton's Bay, Glen Arbor, Empire, Kalkaska, Garfield Twp., Platte Lake, Platte Bay, Honor, Frankfort, Manistee, and Lake

Michigan and the inland areas, the Lake Michigan side of the Northern LP has numerous unique tourist spots, places to find great food, lighthouses, marinas, good boating, fishing, any type of outdoor sport or event, and festivals. Have you ever swam in Lake Michigan on a hot summer day after working in the hot summer sun in "putting up hay bales" on a wagon all day? I did that as a teenager. We would go to Lake Michigan after the work was done and swim. What a treat that was back then, I call it the "old days" of my youth. I remember good times spent at Lake Michigan in all seasons of the year. All over this side of the "mitten" there are state forest areas, campgrounds, nature preserves, harbors, light houses, hiking and walking trails, vacation spots. One unique place is The Tunnel of Trees near Harbor Springs. This is a beautiful spot in the fall season. There is a Heritage Route, Five Mile Creek Nature Preserve, Harbor Springs Vineyards & Winery to name a few of the places to visit in this area. All along the Lake Michigan shoreline there are small islands and beaches and places to stop and visit. Inland are more great places to explore. In any season, this area of the state provides hundreds of interesting tourist attractions, events, festivals, and great food. Too many to list, I will try to highlight a few of them. Stop

>TOURIST

at Little Traverse Bay and Harbor Point and visit Little Traverse Lighthouse. Visit Fisherman's Island State Park near Charlevoix. Stop and enjoy picturesque Leland with the boats, lighthouse, Good Harbor Bay, Van's Beach, Leland River, and Fishtown. It is a place to spend the weekend. Michigan is a state where you can just pick a spot anywhere in this beautiful state and you will find great people, food, and tourist spots galore. There are many peaceful places to just sit back and enjoy nature's simple beauty found only in beautiful "Pure Michigan".

35. THE SOUTHWEST CORNER OF THE STATE

The SW corner of Michigan offers many cool places to visit. In the old days, I used to hear an old saying "go jump in Lake Michigan". Okay, to cool off, I would like to do that on a hot summer's day. Seriously though, you will like Saugatuck, South Haven, and South Haven's North Beach with year-round lake access with fishing, swimming, concessions, a playground & a pier. Across the river is South Beach which has playgrounds, a pier and a skateboard park. This popular area draws families to this lakefront beach with lighthouse views. The two beach areas are divided by the Black River. There are plenty of condos, beach houses, cottages, Martha's Vineyard Bed & Breakfast, hotels, restaurants, vineyards, several parks, yacht clubs and marinas, boat launches, nature preserves, and lots of family friendly & historic places to visit like Haven Peach Historical Marker at the Stanley Johnston Park which tells about the Haven Peaches and how they were developed by Michigan State University's South Haven Experiment Station under the direction of Professor Stanley Johnston from 1924 to 1963. They developed eight varieties of yellow freestone Haven peaches which are the Halehaven, Kalhaven, Redhaven, Fairhaven, Sunhaven, Richhaven, Glohaven, and Cresthaven. The Redhaven peach was the first commercial peach variety and it is still my favorite. The Redhaven peach is the most widely planted freestone variety in the world. Visit the South Haven Chamber of Commerce to learn interesting facts about this area. Nearby are communities like Fennville, Allegan, Hamilton, Otsego, Plainwell, Bloomingdale, Paw Paw, Mattawan, Gobles, Kendall, Kalamazoo, Battle Creek, Portage, Vicksburg, and many more wonderful communities to visit. Travel farther south to Lake Michigan Beach and the Benton

>TOURIST

Harbor and St. Joseph areas. As you travel south along the shoreline you will see communities like Shoreham, Stevensville, Baroda, Bridgman, New Troy, Union Pier, Three Oaks, New Buffalo, and Grand Beach. Michiana is the city near the Michigan and Indiana border. Farther inland, are Eau Claire, Sodus Township, Berrien Center, Niles, Dowagiac, Decatur, Cassopolis, Edwardsburg, Vandalia, Jones, Union, Williamsville, White Pigeon, Three Rivers, Constantine, and so many more. Personally visiting this area of the state a few times, I can attest that it is beautiful in any season. Especially beautiful is the winter season with the snow on the pine trees along the many creeks, rivers and lakes. Along the Pigeon River and the St. Joseph River area, it is absolutely beautiful. Visit the White Pigeon area in St. Joseph County or travel to Sturgis, Burr Oak, Colon, Bronson, Volinia, Marcellus, with so many great communities in this area, it is difficult to list all of them. Explore this beautiful SW corner of the state.

36. THE MIDDLE AND SOUTH BORDER AREA

Like the SW corner of Michigan, the middle and south border area is equally beautiful and historic with parks, trees, and lakes. In the Coldwater, MI, area there are several parks and lakes, i.e. Branch County Memorial Park, and the Rotary Park. Visit the Little River Railroad, or for old fashioned fun, drive to nearby Capri Drive-Inn Theater. Within this area, are several beautiful ponds, lakes and rivers. For example, Hodunk Pong, Hog Creek, Craig Lake, the Cold Water River, Morrison Lake, Randall Lake, North Lake, Cemetery Lake, Little Long Lake, Messenger Lake, West Long Lake, South Lake, and Cold Creek. Farther south is Coldwater Lake, East Long Lake, and farther north is Archer Lake, Middle Lake, Fisher Creek, Lake Hanchet, and Marble Lake. All combined it makes a water paradise for anyone who likes to swim, fish, kayak, or canoe. What a beautiful scenic area of the state. There are plenty of businesses that service this area like Cottonwood Resort, Brad's Cottage, Boaters Marine, Middle Lake Boat Launch, Sunset Cove Resort, and Quincy Golf Course. Add to that thousands of restaurants, golf courses, retail stores, and every major convenience imaginable. Surrounding communities, to name a few, are Girard, Union City, Sherwood, Allen, Reading, Litchfield, Jonesville, Mosherville, North Adams, Hillsdale, Osseo, Pittsford, Shadyside, Montgomery (near the corner border of Michigan and

>TOURIST

Indiana). In this spot visit Long Lake which is split in the middle between the two states of Michigan and Indiana. Travel farther east to Camden and Austin (near the Michigan and Ohio state line), and farther north is Frontier, Waldron, Pittsford, Pratville, and Hudson in Lenawee County and nearby Lake Hudson Recreation Area. Farther north and east is Morenci, Clayton, Cadmus, Adrian, Madison Charter Twp., Blissfield, Ottawa Lake, and farther north is Cement City, Manchester, Saline, Ypsilanti, Chelsea, Jackson, Michigan Center, Spring Arbor, and Ann Arbor. I could go on forever about how many wonderful places there are in this part of the state.

37. THE MICHIGAN AND TOLEDO, OH, BORDER AREA

Personally, I have driven through this area of the state numerous times traveling south more than 40 times driving down the I-75 (Detroit-Toledo Expy) and US 23 corridor area of the state. Stop in Luna Pier, Grand View, Ottawa Lake, Temperance, Samaria, Lambertville, or Erie, MI, on the Lake Erie and SE corner of the state. In this area are communities like Adrian, Madison Charter Twp., Sand Creek, Cadmus, Ogden, Blissfield, and Riga.

Farther northwest is Jackson and farther northeast is Ann Arbor and Detroit. Visit Dundee, Azalia, Britton, Milan, Tecumseh, Maybee, Steiner, Petersburg, Ida, Raisinville Twp., Monroe, Oakville, Flat Rock, Gross Ile, Woodhaven, and Southgate. Remember as you are traveling south on I-75 to stop in Toledo for a Toledo Mudhens baseball game. The Toledo Mudhens, founded in 1883, play at Fifth Third Field which is located in downtown Toledo nearby to the Maumee River. They are a Triple-A team affiliated with the Detroit Tigers which is an MLB team. I am a big Detroit Tigers fan. Stop and grab a bite to eat in Luna Pier. The City of Luna Pier and Public Beach and Pier offer a nice view of Lake Erie and the city is six miles northeast of the Michigan-Ohio border. And just north is Water Tower Park at Allens Cove another good area is Grand View. All along the shoreline from Gross Ile south to the state line are tourist areas with interesting places, hotels, and restaurants with good food and nice people where you can stop to catch a view of beautiful Lake Erie.

The Top Products and Industries produced in Michigan.

>TOURIST

38. AGRICULTURE

Twenty-four percent (24%) of Michigan's agriculture revenues are from dairy products, i.e., milk, and cheese and it ranks as #2 among all of the U.S. states. For livestock, cattle, calves, hogs, chickens, eggs, and turkeys are important with several large chick and turkey hatcheries located within the state.

39. CROPS

Greenhouse and nursery products (trees, flowers, shrubbery) generate 14% of total agricultural revenues. Michigan is the 2nd largest national producer of Christmas trees. Corn for grain comprises 11% of agricultural revenue. Other vegetable crops are asparagus, bell peppers, carrots, celery, cucumbers, onions, potatoes, pumpkins, snap beans, sweet corn, and tomatoes. Major crops include soybeans, sugar beets, wheat, and hay. Michigan is a leading producer of apples, blueberries, rhubarb, and cherries from Traverse City, MI. Anything cherry, Yum!

40. MANUFACTURING, TRANSPORTATION, PRODUCTION

Manufacturing, Transportation, Production of machinery (bearings, chisels, dies, valves, machine parts, computers, conveyors, engines, machine tools, and pumps is the second-ranked sector), Fabricated metal products, i.e. cutlery, hand tools, and hardware rank third for revenue. Michigan is the leading with manufacturing of sporting goods and athletic equipment.

41. MINING

Natural gas, iron ore, and petroleum. The world's largest limestone quarry (Michigan Limestone and Chemical, Co.) is located near Rogers City, Michigan. Stop here, it looks like a tiny Grand Canyon and it is a cool place to visit for an interesting weekend tourist trip. Michigan is the leading producer of iron oxide pigments and magnesium compounds in the USA as well as a leader in producing gypsum, iodine, peat, sand, and gravel. Expensive to mine, large deposits of copper still exist here.

>TOURIST

42. FISHING

Great Lakes fishing is the best! Whitefish, lake trout, lake herring, salmon, yellow perch, catfish, and chubs are popular. Each spring, smelt is very popular to catch from Michigan's streams and rivers.

43. SERVICES

Michigan has hundreds of community, business, and personal services, i.e., private health care, law offices, engineering and research companies, repair shops, and computer software companies which make services a leading industry for the state.

44. INDUSTRY

Michigan's major industries are manufacturing, tourism, and agriculture. Anywhere you stand in Michigan, you are 85 miles from a Great Lake. Spanning the Straits of Mackinac, the Mackinac Bridge, part of I-75, is the third longest suspension bridge in the USA.

45. WHAT FAMOUS PRODUCTS CAME FROM MICHIGAN?

Below are but a few of the many famous products originating as the best Michigan-made food products you didn't know existed. Years ago, Detroit was once the potato chip capital and also famous for beer companies who originated in Detroit. Some well-known brands from Michigan include: Dave's Sweet Tooth Toffee, Mindo Chocolate, Detroit Bold Coffee, Velvet Peanut Butter, Great Lakes Potato Chips, Cherry Republic Products, McClure's Pickles, Germack Pistachio Nuts and products, Hudsonville Creamery & Ice Cream Company (Superman aka Super Scoop version), Superior Thaw, Tiger Traxx, and Grand Hotel Pecan Ball are famous favorites produced by Hudsonville). Superman Ice Cream is "a Michigan thing" and a Midwest favorite with several companies producing their version of this favorite ice cream. An internet search will reveal a variety of sources from which Superman Ice Cream originated. More great favorites produced in Michigan include (not a finite list) McClure's potato chips, pickles, relish, and other products. More products include: Vlasic brand, Original Murdick's Mackinac Island Fudge, Bon Bon Bon Chocolates (Alex Clark's fancy treats), Garden Fresh Gourmet brand, Better Made brand, Kellogg's brand products, Gerber baby food products, Faygo, Vernors (two of my favorites "pop" soft drinks). More products include Aunt Jane's Pickles, and Pioneer / Michigan Sugar. Other items originating in Michigan: Fiber Optics, the Automobile Assembly Line, Baby Food (Gerber), Jiffy Mix baking mix (corn muffin and pie crust), Kellogg's Cereal (Battle Creek, MI), paved yellow road lines, penicillin production, early modern traffic signals, Vernors Ginger Ale (Detroit, MI), and hospital beds. There are thousands of products that originated in Michigan. I wish I could list them all. Michigan-made products have a long and proud history. Detroit was once a major player in the pickle industry. Michigan's entrepreneurial spirit and creative people are what has made Michigan a leader of business and tourism.

46. MICHIGAN WINE, BEER, CIDER

Michigan has more than 325 craft beer breweries, more than 120 microbreweries and brewpubs. According to 2016/2017 figures, Michigan has 13,700 acres of vineyards and wineries making it the fourth largest grape-growing state. Michigan leads in the top ten USA states for wine grape production. Annually, Michigan commercial wineries produce more than 2.7 million gallons of wine making it the top as fifth in USA wine production with the majority coming from Michigan-grown grapes. Michigan wineries attract more than 1.7 million tourists. Most quality wine grapes grow within 25 miles of Lake Michigan. Red Delicious, Golden Delicious, Gala and Honey Crisp, Paula Red, Winesapp apples and more abound at more than 100 historic Michigan cider mills where you can watch the cider-making process. Yates Cider Mill has been in operation since 1863 in Rochester Hills, MI. Make a day of it; take the family to Uncle John's Cider Mill near St. Johns, MI, in business since the 1900's. Buy pumpkins and go on a hayride and they have a five-acre corn maze. Here are a few more cider mills to visit: Blake's Orchard in Armada, MI; Parshallville Grist Mill and Cider Mill in Fenton,

>TOURIST

MI; Franklin Cider Mill is north of downtown Detroit; Dexter Cider Mill near Ann Arbor, MI.

47. APPLES, BLUEBERRIES, AND CHERRIES

Northern Michigan has its cherries with Traverse City as famous for everything cherry, but the western coast of the state, on the shores of Lake Michigan, is all about the blueberries. Travel inland and you will find many locales with blueberries. Michigan is also known for its Redhaven peaches. In addition, Michigan growers produce other fruit crops such as apples, peaches, pears, plums, grapes, raspberries, strawberries, and rhubarb. Michigan is the third largest grower of field-grown rhubarb. Fruit is abundant, delicious, nutritious, great to bake and eat, and hard to beat! Yum, apple, cherry, blueberry, peach, and rhubarb pie!

48. THE TOP 5 REASONS TO VISIT MICHIGAN

I could think of many more reasons to visit this beautiful gem that is the only state in the USA with two peninsulas and five freshwater Great Lakes.

(1) Sleeping Bear Dunes National Lakeshore, on the shore of Lake Michigan, was rated as one of the most beautiful places in the USA., (2) Ann Arbor, (3) Mackinaw Island, (4) Great place for all types of sports, (5) Pictured Rocks National Lakeshore.

49. MORE MICHIGAN-MADE PRODUCTS

Not a finite list, below are but a few of the products made in Michigan.

There are thousands of items produced showing the "Michigan Mitten".

Arts & Crafts products, Auto Products: Auto Detailing, Brake Care, Decals, Helmet Care, Key chains, Tire Detailing, Visor Care

Bath & Body: Aromatherapy, Baby & Kids, Bath & Spa, Lip Care, Men's care products, Nail Care, Skin Care

>TOURIST

Collectibles: Glassware, Gumball Machines, Keepsakes, Decorative Magnets, Mugs, Ornaments, Pottery & Ceramics

Fashion: Apparel (Ladies & Men), Bags & Wallets, Children's, Head & Foot Wear, Jewelry, Outerwear

Food Products: Baked Goods, Beverages, Candy & Sweets, Cherry Products, Jams, Maple Syrup, Salsa & Sauces, Snacks, Spices, Superman Ice Cream

Hunting and Fishing related products

Household Products: Bathroom, Fragrance, Home Decor, Kitchen & Dining, Lighting, Ornaments, Utility, Yard & Garden

Media Products: Books, Calendars, Cookbooks, CD's & DVD's, Gift Tags & Paper, Cards, Decals & Stickers, Journals, Posters & Prints

Pet Products: Aquarium Signs, Pet Art, Pet Fashion, Pet Food, Pet Grooming, Pet Journals, Pet Toys

Toys & Hobbies: Activity Books, Aquarium Signs, Dolls, Games, Golf, Journals, Turkey & Deer Patch Posters

Wine Theme & Beer products: Gifts for Her, Gifts for Him, Michigan Theme

Reference: Do a Google search for Michigan-Made.com or Michigan Products

50. MICHIGAN CITIES WITH SIGNATURE FOOD

Michigan is a great state to visit to sample a variety of food. All over the state from the LP
to the UP, you will find unique food to savor and then want more.

Battle Creek - cereal- nicknamed Cereal City

Detroit – coney dog

Frankenmuth – chicken – Zehnders's and Bavarian Inn

Grand Rapids – wet burrito

Hamtramck – Paczki (Polish pastry – ref: Fat Tuesday)

Mackinaw Island – fudge

Northern Michigan - Whitefish

Saginaw – steak sandwich

Sparta – apples (Fruit Ridge: Their annual apple festival is in September.)

South Haven - blueberries

Traverse City - cherries

The Upper Peninsula (UP) – Northern Pasty (originated with Cornish miners)

West Michigan – olive burger

>TOURIST

It should be noted that all over Michigan, in both the UP and LP, there are great places to go for food and beverages, like Pinconning for cheese, and all over the state there are apples, berries of all types, mint in St. Johns – reference the annual St. Johns Mint Festival held in August. Or, try the famous Detroit style pizza. There is a Maple Syrup Festival in Shepherd, MI. Michigan is famous for Faygo and Vernors. Also, Koegel's hotdogs and bologna, lake fish, Double-baked Rye Bread, Greek Salad, Germack Pistachio nuts, Mooney's Ice Cream, Better Made chips, cider and doughnuts, Greek salad, Polish, German, and Italian food. Michigan has any type of ethnic food you could ever want.

>TOURIST

TOP REASONS TO BOOK THIS TRIP

Michigan is my birthplace, and I want to share with everyone what a beautiful place it is to visit. I love the changing of the seasons, winter, spring, summer, and fall. Every season in Michigan is a treasure to behold. I have wonderful memories of good times spent there. Take a fall color tour to see the beautiful gold, red, and yellow leaves and take a boat ride to see the Pictured Rocks. Sit out at night under the stars and roast marshmallows by a campfire. You are never too old to catch fireflies. On rare occasions witness and experience the breathtaking northern lights. Walk in new fallen snow in December and you will love to spend the Christmas holiday season in a winter wonderland. See the tulips in the spring at Holland, MI. Go to the Cherry Festival in June. You will love the natural beauty of the state, the Five Great Lakes, the music, food, culture, great places to visit, and nice people to meet. You will absolutely love magical Pure Michigan!

Lighthouses and beaches: The lighthouses here are the best.

Food: The food is amazing. Michigan has rich cultural heritage.

Island, lake, and peninsula culture linked with tradition.

>TOURIST

BONUS BOOK

50 THINGS TO KNOW ABOUT PACKING LIGHT FOR TRAVEL

PACK THE RIGHT WAY EVERY TIME

AUTHOR: MANIDIPA BHATTACHARYYA

First Published in 2015 by Dr. Lisa Rusczyk. Copyright 2015. All Rights Reserved. No part of this publication may be reproduced, including scanning and photocopying, or distributed in any form or by any means, electronic or mechanical, or stored in a database or retrieval system without prior written permission from the publisher.

Disclaimer: The publisher has put forth an effort in preparing and arranging this book. The information provided herein by the author is provided "as is". Use this information at your own risk. The publisher is not a licensed doctor. Consult your doctor before engaging in any medical activities. The publisher and author disclaim any liabilities for any loss of profit or commercial or personal damages resulting from the information contained in this book.

Edited by Melanie Howthorne

ABOUT THE AUTHOR

Manidipa Bhattacharyya is a creative writer and editor, with an education in English literature and Linguistics. After working in the IT industry for seven long years she decided to call it quits and follow her heart instead. Manidipa has been ghost writing, editing, proof reading and doing secondary research services for many story tellers and article writers for about three years. She stays in Kolkata, India with her husband and a busy two year old. In her own time Manidipa enjoys travelling, photography and writing flash fiction.

Manidipa believes in travelling light and never carries anything that she couldn't haul herself on a trip. However, travelling with her child changed the scenario. She seemed to carry the entire world with her for the baby on the first two trips. But good sense prevailed and she is again working her way to becoming a light traveler, this time with a kid.

INTRODUCTION

*He who would travel happily
must travel light.*

-Antoine de Saint-Exupéry

Travel takes you to different places from seas and mountains to deserts and much more. In your travels you get to interact with different people and their cultures. You will, however, enjoy the sights and interact positively with these new people even more, if you are travelling light.

When you travel light your mind can be free from worry about your belongings. You do not have to spend precious vacation time waiting for your luggage to arrive after a long flight. There is be no chance of your bags going missing and the best part is that you need not pay a fee for checked baggage.

People who have mastered this art of packing light will root for you to take only one carry-on, wherever you go. However, many people can find it really hard to pack light. More so if you are travelling with children. Differentiating between "must have" and "just in case" items is the starting point. There will be ample shopping avenues at your destination which are just waiting to be explored.

This book will show you 'packing' in a new 'light' – pun intended – and help you to embrace light packing practices for all of your future travels.

Off to packing!

DEDICATION

I dedicate this book to all the travel buffs that I know, who have given me great insights into the contents of their backpacks.

THE RIGHT TRAVEL GEAR

1. CHOOSE YOUR TRAVEL GEAR CAREFULLY

While selecting your travel gear, pick items that are light weight, durable and most importantly, easy to carry. There are cases with wheels so you can drag them along – these are usually on the heavy side because of the trolley. Alternatively a backpack that you can carry comfortably on your back, or even a duffel bag that you can carry easily by hand or sling across your body are also great options. Whatever you choose, one thing to keep in mind is that the luggage itself should not weigh a ton, this will give you the flexibility to bring along one extra pair of shoes if you so desire.

\>TOURIST

2. CARRY THE MINIMUM NUMBER OF BAGS

Selecting light weight luggage is not everything. You need to restrict the number of bags you carry as well. One carry-on size bag is ideal for light travel. Most carriers allow one cabin baggage plus one purse, handbag or camera bag as long as it slides under the seat in front. So technically, you can carry two items of luggage without checking them in.

3. PACK ONE EXTRA BAG

Always pack one extra empty bag along with your essential items. This could be a very light weight duffel bag or even a sturdy tote bag which takes up minimal space. In the event that you end up buying a lot of souvenirs, you already have a handy bag to stuff all that into and do not have to spend time hunting for an appropriate bag.

I'm very strict with my packing and have everything in its right place. I never change a rule. I hardly use anything in the hotel room. I wheel my own wardrobe in and that's it.

Charlie Watts

CLOTHES & ACCESSORIES

4. PLAN AHEAD

Figure out in advance what you plan to do on your trip. That will help you to pick that one dress you need for the occasion. If you are going to attend a wedding then you have to carry formal wear. If not, you can ditch the gown for something lighter that will be comfortable during long walks or on the beach.

5. WEAR THAT JACKET

Remember that wearing items will not add extra luggage for your air travel. So wear that bulky jacket that you plan to carry for your trip. This saves space and can also help keep you warm during the chilly flight.

6. MIX AND MATCH

Carry clothes that can be interchangeably used to reinvent your look. Find one top that goes well with a couple of pairs of pants or skirts. Use tops, shirts and jackets wisely along with other accessories like a scarf or a stole to create a new look.

7. CHOOSE YOUR FABRIC WISELY

Stuffing clothes in cramped bags definitely takes its toll which results in wrinkles. It is best to carry wrinkle free, synthetic clothes or merino tops. This will eliminate the need for that small iron you usually bring along.

8. DITCH CLOTHES PACK UNDERWEAR

Pack more underwear and socks. These are the things that will give you a fresh feel even if you do not get a chance to wear fresh clothes. Moreover these are easy to wash and can be dried inside the hotel room itself.

9. CHOOSE DARK OVER LIGHT

While picking your clothes choose dark coloured ones. They are easy to colour coordinate and can last longer before needing a wash. Accidental food spills and dirt from the road are less visible on darker clothes.

10. WEAR YOUR JEANS

Take only one pair of Jeans with you, which you should wear on the flight. Remember to pick a pair that can be worn for sightseeing trips and is equally eloquent for dinner. You can add variety by adding light weight cargoes and chinos.

11. CARRY SMART ACCESSORIES

The right accessory can give you a fresh look even with the same old dress. An intelligent neck-piece, a couple of bright scarves, stoles or a sarong can be used in a number of ways to add variety to your clothing. These light weight beauties can double up as a nursing cover, a light blanket, beach wear, a modesty cover for visiting places of worship, and also makes for an enthralling game of peek-a-boo.

12. LEARN TO FOLD YOUR GARMENTS

Seasoned travellers all swear by rolling their clothes for compact and wrinkle free packing. Bundle packing, where you roll the clothes around a central object as if tying it up, is also a popular method of compact and wrinkle free packing. Stacking folded clothes one on top of another is a big no-no as it makes creases extreme and they are difficult to get rid of without ironing.

13. WASH YOUR DIRTY LAUNDRY

One of the ways to avoid carrying loads of clothes is to wash the clothes you carry. At some places you might get to use the laundry services or a Laundromat but if you are in a pinch, best solution is to wash them yourself. If that is the plan then carrying quick drying clothes is highly recommended, which most often also happen to be the wrinkle free variety.

14. LEAVE THOSE TOWELS BEHIND

Regular towels take up a lot of space, are heavy and take ages to dry out. If you are staying at hotels they will provide you with towels anyway. If you are travelling to a remote place, where the availability of towels look doubtful, carry a light weight travel towel of viscose material to do the job.

15. USE A COMPRESSION BAG

Compression bags are getting lots of recommendation now days from regular travellers. These are useful for saving space in your luggage when you have to pack bulky dresses. While packing for the return trip, get help from the hotel staff to arrange a vacuum cleaner.

FOOTWEAR

16. PUT ON YOUR HIKING BOOTS

If you have plans to go hiking or trekking during your trip, you will need those bulky hiking boots. The best way to carry them is to wear them on flight to save space and luggage weight. You can remove the boots once inside and be comfortable in your socks.

17. PICKING THE RIGHT SHOES

Shoes are often the bulkiest items, along with being the dainty if you are a female. They need care and take up a lot of space in your luggage. It is advisable therefore to pick shoes very carefully. If you plan to do a lot of walking and site seeing, then wearing a pair of comfortable walking shoes are a must. For more formal occasions you can carry durable, light weight flats which will not take up much space.

18. STUFF SHOES

If you happen to pack a pair of shoes, ensure you utilize their hollow insides. Tuck small items like rolled up socks or belts to save space. They will also be easy to find.

TOILETRIES

19. STASHING TOILETRIES

Carry only absolute necessities. Airline rules dictate that for one carry-on bag, liquids and gels must be in 3.4 ounce (100ml) bottles or less, and must be packed in a one quart zip-lock bag. If you are planning to stay in a hotel, the basic things will be provided for you. It's best is to buy the rest from the local market at your destination.

20. TAKE ALONG TAMPONS

Tampons are a hard to find item in a lot of countries. Figure out how many you need and pack accordingly. For longer stays you can buy them online and have them delivered to where you are staying.

21. GET PAMPERED BEFORE YOU TRAVEL

Some avid travellers suggest getting a pedicure and manicure just the day before travelling. This not only gives you a well kept look, you also save the trouble of packing nail polish. Remember, every little bit of weight reduced adds up.

ELECTRONICS

22. LUGGING ALONG ELECTRONICS

Electronics have a large role to play in our lives today. Most of us cannot imagine our lives away from our phones, laptops or tablets. However while travelling, one must consider the amount of weight these electronics add to our luggage. Thankfully smart phones come along with all the essentials tools like a camera, email access, picture editing tools and more. They are smart to the point of eliminating the need to carry multiple gadgets. Choose a smart phone that suits all your requirements and travel with the world in your palms or pocket.

23. REDUCE THE NUMBER OF CHARGERS

If you do travel with multiple electronic devices, you will have to bear the additional burden of carrying all their chargers too. Check if a single charger can be used for multiple devices. You might also consider investing in a pocket charger. These small devices support multiple devices while keeping you charged on the go.

>TOURIST

24. TRAVEL FRIENDLY APPS

Along with smart phones come numerous apps, which are immensely helpful in our travels. You name it and you have an app for it at hand – take pictures, sharing with friends and family, torch to light dark roads, maps, checking flight/train times, find hotels and many other things. Use these smart alternatives to traditional items like books to eliminate weight and save space.

I get ideas about what's essential when packing my suitcase.

-Diane von Furstenberg

TRAVELLING WITH KIDS

25. BRING ALONG THE STROLLER

Kids might enjoy walking for a while but they soon tire out and a stroller is the just the right thing for them to rest in while you continue your tour. Strollers also double duty as a luggage carrier and shopping bag holder. Remember to pick a light weight, easy to handle brand of stroller. Better yet, find out in advance if you can rent a stroller at your destination.

26. BRING ONLY ENOUGH DIAPERS FOR YOUR TRIP

Diapers take up a lot of space and add to the weight of your luggage. Therefore it is advisable to carry just enough diapers to last through the trip and a few for afterwards, till you buy fresh stock at your destination. Unless of course you are travelling to a really remote area, in which case you have no choice but to carry the load. Otherwise diapers are something you will find pretty easily.

27. TAKE ONLY A COUPLE OF TOYS

Children are easily attracted by new things in their environment. While travelling they will find numerous 'new' objects to scrutinize and play with. Packing just one favorite toy is enough, or if there is no favorite toy leave out all of them in favor of stories or imaginary games.

28. CARRY KID FRIENDLY SNACKS

Create a small snack counter in your bag to store away quick bites for those sudden hunger pangs. Depending on the child's age this could include chocolates, raisins, dry fruits, granola bars or biscuits. Also keep a bottle of water handy for your little one.

These things do not add much weight and can be adjusted in a handbag or knapsack.

29. GAMES TO CARRY

Create some travel specific, imaginary games if you have slightly grown up children, like spot the attractions. Keep a coloring book and colors handy for in-flight or hotel time. Apps on your smart phone can keep the children engaged with cartoons and story books. Older children are often entertained by games available on phones or tablets. This cuts the weight of luggage down while keeping the kids entertained.

30. LET THE KIDS CARRY THEIR LOAD

A good thing is to start early sharing of responsibilities. Let your child pick a bag of his or her choice and pack it themselves. Keep tabs on what they are stuffing in their bags by asking if they will be using that item on the trip. It could start out being just an entertainment bag initially but with growing years they will learn to sort the useful from the superfluous. Children as little as four can maneuver a small trolley suitcase like a pro- their experience in pull along toys credit. If you are worried that you may be pulling it for them, you may want to start with a backpack.

31. DECIDE ON LOCATION FOR CHILDREN TO SLEEP

While on a trip you might not always get a crib at your destination, and carrying one will make life all the more difficult. Instead call ahead to see if there are any cribs or roll out beds for children. You may even put blankets on the floor. Weave them a story about camping and they will gladly sleep without any trouble.

32. GET BABY PRODUCTS DELIVERED AT YOUR DESTINATION

If you are absolutely paranoid about not getting your favourite variety of diaper or brand of baby food, check out online stores like amazon.com for services in your destination city. You can buy things online ahead of your travel and get them delivered to your hotel upon arrival.

33. FEEDING NEEDS OF YOUR INFANTS

If you are travelling with a breastfed infant, you save the trouble of carrying bottles and bottle sanitization kits. For special food, or medications, you may need to call ahead to make sure you have a refrigerator where you are staying.

34. FEEDING NEEDS OF YOUR TODDLER

With the progression from infancy to toddler, their dietary requirements too evolve. You will have to pack some snacks for travelling time. Fresh fruits and vegetables can be purchased at your destination. Most of the cities you travel to in whichever part of the world, will have baby food products and formulas, available at the local drug-store or the supermarket.

35. PICKING CLOTHES FOR YOUR BABY

Contrary to popular belief, babies can do without many changes of clothes. At the most pack 2 outfits per day. Pack mix and match type clothes for your little one as well. Pick things which are comfortable to wear and quick to dry.

36. SELECTING SHOES FOR YOUR BABY

Like outfits, kids can make do with two pairs of comfortable shoes. If you can get some water resistant shoes it will be best. To expedite drying wet shoes, you can stuff newspaper in them then wrap them with newspaper and leave them to dry overnight.

37. KEEP ONE CHANGE OF CLOTHES HANDY

Travelling with kids can be tricky. Keep a change of clothes for the kids and mum handy in your purse or tote bag. This takes a bit of space in your hand luggage but comes extremely handy in case there are any accidents or spills.

38. LEAVE BEHIND BABY ACCESSORIES

Baby accessories like their bed, bath tub, car seat, crib etc. should be left at home. Many hotels provide a crib on request, while car seats can be borrowed from friends or rented. Babies can be given a bath in the hotel sink or even in the adult bath tub with a little bit of water. If you bring a few bath toys, they can be used in the bath, pool, and out of water. They can also be sanitized easily in the sink.

39. CARRY A SMALL LOAD OF PLASTIC BAGS

With children around there are chances of a number of soiled clothes and diapers. These plastic bags help to sort the dirt from the clean inside your big bag.

These are very light weight and come in handy to other carry stuff as well at times.

PACK WITH A PURPOSE

40. PACKING FOR BUSINESS TRIPS

One neutral-colored suit should suffice. It can be paired with different shirts, ties and accessories for different occasions. One pair of black suit pants could be worn with a matching jacket for the office or with a snazzy top for dinner.

41. PACKING FOR A CRUISE

Most cruises have formal dinners, and that formal dress usually takes up a lot of space. However you might find a tuxedo to rent. For women, a short black dress with multiple accessory options will do the trick.

42. PACKING FOR A LONG TRIP OVER DIFFERENT CLIMATES

The secret packing mantra for travel over multiple climates is layering. Layering traps air around your body creating insulation against the cold. The same light t-shirt that is comfortable in a warmer climate can be the innermost layer in a colder climate.

REDUCE SOME MORE WEIGHT

43. LEAVE PRECIOUS THINGS AT HOME

Things that you would hate to lose or get damaged leave them at home. Precious jewelry, expensive gadgets or dresses, could be anything. You will not require these on your trip. Leave them at home and spare the load on your mind.

44. SEND SOUVENIRS BY MAIL

If you have spent all your money on purchasing souvenirs, carrying them back in the same bag that you brought along would be difficult. Either pack everything in another bag and check it in the airport or get everything shipped to your home. Use an international carrier for a secure transit, but this could be more expensive than the checking fees at the airport.

45. AVOID CARRYING BOOKS

Books equal to weight. There are many reading apps which you can download on your smart phone or tab.

Plus there are gadgets like Kindle and Nook that are thinner and lighter alternatives to your regular book.

CHECK, GET, SET, CHECK AGAIN

46. STRATEGIZE BEFORE PACKING

Create a travel list and prepare all that you think you need to carry along. Keep everything on your bed or floor before packing and then think through once again – do I really need that? Any item that meets this question can be avoided. Remove whatever you don't really need and pack the rest.

47. TEST YOUR LUGGAGE

Once you have fully packed for the trip take a test trip with your luggage. Take your bags and go to town for window shopping for an hour. If you enjoy your hour long trip it is good to go, if not, go home and reduce the load some more. Repeat this test till you hit the right weight.

48. ADD A ROLL OF DUCT TAPE

You might wonder why, when this book has been talking about reducing stuff, we're suddenly asking you to pack something totally unusual. This is because when you have limited supplies, duct tape is immensely helpful for small repairs – a broken bag, leaking zip-lock bag, broken sunglasses, you name it and duct tape can fix it, temporarily.

49. LIST OF ESSENTIAL ITEMS

Even though the emphasis is on packing light, there are things which have to be carried for any trip. Here is our list of essentials:

- Passport/Visa or any other ID

- Any other paper work that might be required on a trip like permits, hotel reservation confirmations etc.

- Medicines – all your prescription medicines and emergency kit, especially if you are travelling with children

- Medical or vaccination records

- Money in foreign currency if travelling to a different country

- Tickets- Email or Message them to your phone

>TOURIST

50. MAKE THE MOST OF YOUR TRIP

Wherever you are going, whatever you hope to do we encourage you to embrace it whole-heartedly. Take in the scenery, the culture and above all, enjoy your time away from home.

On a long journey even a straw weighs heavy.

-Spanish Proverb

>TOURIST
PACKING AND PLANNING TIPS

A Week before Leaving

- Arrange for someone to take care of pets and water plants.
- Stop mail and newspaper.
- Notify Credit Card companies where you are going.
- Change your thermostat settings.
- Car inspected, oil is changed, and tires have the correct pressure.
- Passports and photo identification is up to date.
- Pay bills.
- Copy important items and download travel Apps.
- Start collecting small bills for tips.

Right Before Leaving

- Clean out refrigerator.
- Empty garbage cans.
- Lock windows.
- Make sure you have the proper identification with you.
- Bring cash for tips.
- Remember travel documents.
- Lock door behind you.
- Remember wallet.
- Unplug items in house and pack chargers.

>TOURIST

READ OTHER GREATER THAN A TOURIST BOOKS

Greater Than a Tourist San Miguel de Allende Guanajuato Mexico: 50 Travel Tips from a Local by Tom Peterson

Greater Than a Tourist – Lake George Area New York USA: 50 Travel Tips from a Local by Janine Hirschklau

Greater Than a Tourist – Monterey California United States: 50 Travel Tips from a Local by Katie Begley

Greater Than a Tourist – Chanai Crete Greece: 50 Travel Tips from a Local by Dimitra Papagrigoraki

Greater Than a Tourist – The Garden Route Western Cape Province South Africa: 50 Travel Tips from a Local by Li-Anne McGregor van Aardt

Greater Than a Tourist – Sevilla Andalusia Spain: 50 Travel Tips from a Local by Gabi Gazon

Greater Than a Tourist – Kota Bharu Kelantan Malaysia: 50 Travel Tips from a Local by Aditi Shukla

Children's Book: Charlie the Cavalier Travels the World by Lisa Rusczyk

>TOURIST

> TOURIST

Visit Greater Than a Tourist for Free Travel Tips
http://GreaterThanATourist.com

Sign up for the Greater Than a Tourist Newsletter for discount days, new books, and travel information:
http://eepurl.com/cxspyf

Follow us on Facebook for tips, images, and ideas:
https://www.facebook.com/GreaterThanATourist

Follow us on Pinterest for travel tips and ideas:
http://pinterest.com/GreaterThanATourist

Follow us on Instagram for beautiful travel images:
http://Instagram.com/GreaterThanATourist

>TOURIST

> TOURIST

Please leave your honest review of this book on Amazon and Goodreads. Please send your feedback to GreaterThanaTourist@gmail.com as we continue to improve the series. We appreciate your positive and constructive feedback. Thank you.

>TOURIST

METRIC CONVERSIONS

TEMPERATURE

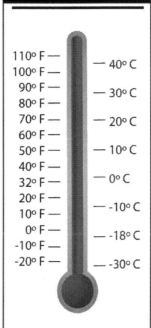

110° F — — 40° C
100° F —
90° F — — 30° C
80° F —
70° F — — 20° C
60° F —
50° F — — 10° C
40° F —
32° F — — 0° C
20° F —
10° F — — -10° C
0° F — — -18° C
-10° F —
-20° F — — -30° C

To convert F to C:

Subtract 32, and then multiply by 5/9 or .5555.

To Convert C to F:
Multiply by 1.8
and then add 32.

32F = 0C

LIQUID VOLUME

To Convert:................Multiply by
U.S. Gallons to Liters................. 3.8
U.S. Liters to Gallons 26
Imperial Gallons to U.S. Gallons 1.2
Imperial Gallons to Liters....... 4.55
Liters to Imperial Gallons 22
1 Liter = .26 U.S. Gallon
1 U.S. Gallon = 3.8 Liters

DISTANCE

To convert ....Multiply by
Inches to Centimeters 2.54
Centimeters to Inches 39
Feet to Meters........................ .3
Meters to Feet 3.28
Yards to Meters 91
Meters to Yards 1.09
Miles to Kilometers 1.61
Kilometers to Miles............ .62
1 Mile = 1.6 km
1 km = .62 Miles

WEIGHT

1 Ounce = .28 Grams
1 Pound = .4555 Kilograms
1 Gram = .04 Ounce
1 Kilogram = 2.2 Pounds

\>TOURIST

TRAVEL QUESTIONS

- Do you bring presents home to family or friends after a vacation?
- Do you get motion sick?
- Do you have a favorite billboard?
- Do you know what to do if there is a flat tire?
- Do you like a sun roof open?
- Do you like to eat in the car?
- Do you like to wear sun glasses in the car?
- Do you like toppings on your ice cream?
- Do you use public bathrooms?
- Did you bring your cell phone and does it have power?
- Do you have a form of identification with you?
- Have you ever been pulled over by a cop?
- Have you ever given money to a stranger on a road trip?
- Have you ever taken a road trip with animals?
- Have you ever went on a vacation alone?
- Have you ever run out of gas?

- If you could move to any place in the world, where would it be?
- If you could travel anywhere in the world, where would you travel?
- If you could travel in any vehicle, which one would it be?
- If you had three things to wish for from a magic genie, what would they be?
- If you have a driver's license, how many times did it take you to pass the test?
- What are you the most afraid of on vacation?
- What do you want to get away from the most when you are on vacation?
- What foods smells bad to you?
- What item do you bring on ever trip with you away from home?
- What makes you sleepy?
- What song would you love to hear on the radio when you're cruising on the highway?
- What travel job would you want the least?
- What will you miss most while you are away from home?
- What is something you always wanted to try?

>TOURIST

- What is the best road side attraction that you ever saw?
- What is the farthest distance you ever biked?
- What is the farthest distance you ever walked?
- What is the weirdest thing you needed to buy while on vacation?
- What is your favorite candy?
- What is your favorite color car?
- What is your favorite family vacation?
- What is your favorite food?
- What is your favorite gas station drink or food?
- What is your favorite license plate design?
- What is your favorite restaurant?
- What is your favorite smell?
- What is your favorite song?
- What is your favorite sound that nature makes?
- What is your favorite thing to bring home from a vacation?
- What is your favorite vacation with friends?
- What is your favorite way to relax?

- Where is the farthest place you ever traveled in a car?
- Where is the farthest place you ever went North, South, East and West?
- Where is your favorite place in the world?
- Who is your favorite singer?
- Who taught you how to drive?
- Who will you miss the most while you are away?
- Who if the first person you will contact when you get to your destination?
- Who brought you on your first vacation?
- Who likes to travel the most in your life?
- Would you rather be hot or cold?
- Would you rather drive above, below, or at the speed limited?
- Would you rather drive on a highway or a back road?
- Would you rather go on a train or a boat?
- Would you rather go to the beach or the woods?

>TOURIST

TRAVEL BUCKET LIST

1.

2.

3.

4.

5.

6.

7.

8.

9.

10.

>TOURIST

NOTES

Made in the USA
Monee, IL
02 December 2019